Women in the
Great War

Women in the Great War

Stephen Wynn

&

Tanya Wynn

Pen & Sword
MILITARY

First published in Great Britain in 2017 by
PEN & SWORD MILITARY
an imprint of
Pen & Sword Books Ltd
47 Church Street
Barnsley
South Yorkshire
S70 2AS

Copyright © Stephen Wynn and Tanya Wynn, 2017

ISBN 978-1-47383-414-9

The right of Stephen Wynn and Tanya Wynn to be identified as the authors of this work has been asserted by them in accordance with the Copyright, Designs and Patents Act 1988.

A CIP catalogue record for this book is available from the British Library.

Typeset by Concept, Huddersfield, West Yorkshire, HD4 5JL.
Printed and bound in England by CPI Group (UK) Ltd, Croydon CR0 4YY.

Pen & Sword Books Ltd incorporates the imprints of Pen & Sword Archaeology, Atlas, Aviation, Battleground, Discovery, Family History, History, Maritime, Military, Naval, Politics, Railways, Select, Social History, Transport, True Crime, and Claymore Press, Frontline Books, Leo Cooper, Praetorian Press, Remember When, Seaforth Publishing and Wharncliffe.

For a complete list of Pen & Sword titles please contact
PEN & SWORD BOOKS LIMITED
47 Church Street, Barnsley, South Yorkshire, S70 2AS, England
E-mail: enquiries@pen-and-sword.co.uk
Website: www.pen-and-sword.co.uk

CONTENTS

ABOUT THE AUTHORS

Stephen and Tanya have been together for the last fourteen years. Initially their shared interest was their four German Shepherd dogs but when Stephen caught the writing bug in 2010, Tanya was a big influence on his first book: *Two Sons in a Warzone – Afghanistan: The True Story of a Father's Conflict*. Stephen kept a diary whilst his sons were both serving in Afghanistan during 2008. But it was just that, a diary, full of his innermost feelings and thoughts, of reading letters, speaking on the telephone and intently watching the evening news. One day whilst on holiday, Tanya suggested 'Why don't you turn it in to a book?' So he took her advice.

After this, Stephen simply never stopped writing. He collaborated with one of his writing partners, Ken Porter, on a book published in August 2012, *German POW Camp 266 – Langdon Hills*, which spent six weeks as the number one best-seller in Waterstones, Basildon in 2013. Stephen and Ken collaborated on a further four books in the Towns & Cities in the Great War series by Pen & Sword. Stephen has also written other titles for the same series.

Since then he has co-written three crime thrillers, published between 2010 and 2012, which feature a fictional detective named Terry Danvers. He has also written a novella based on a Second World War prisoner of war camp which features a mysterious diary.

With this new joint venture, apart from walking their dogs early each morning when most sensible people are still fast asleep, Stephen and Tanya now have another common interest.

CHAPTER ONE

WOMEN IN GENERAL

The First World War, or the Great War as it was initially referred to, was undoubtedly responsible for a big change in the lives of British women, but it was not the sole reason behind their eventual emancipation. There had been many moves made by women to change and improve their lot in life, at all levels of society, as far back as the 1880s.

The Women's Social and Political Union (WSPU), had been founded in 1903 by mother and daughter, Emmeline and Christabel Pankhurst, eleven years before the war started.

Better known as the Suffragettes, they fought for a better life and a better world for women, which was no easy thing to achieve in a time when they were seen by male dominated British society as nothing more than radical campaigners. The politicians of the day, who were all men, had not yet grasped the advantages of embracing women on equal terms and the benefits that would come with such an approach. Instead they used as their excuse for not

Women's Social and Political Union logo.

engaging with or supporting them, the sometimes violent methods employed by the suffragettes to further their cause.

In essence, at the time of the First World War, women were generally regarded as second class citizens, who should know their place in life and, so far as politicians were concerned, were hardly worthy of negotiations or concessions.

With few exceptions, work deemed suitable for women, was associated with domestic service, shop work or the teaching of primary age children. Once a woman had married, not only was she seen as being the property of her husband, but she was expected to stop working, bear him children, look after the home and be a dutiful and obedient wife. At the time the

Emmeline Pankhurst.

word 'obey' was part of a woman's wedding vows and taken more literally than it is today.

History records that the First World War was a massive stepping stone in the long and sometime arduous journey towards equality for women, in all aspects of social and domestic life. The suffrage movement was

Christabel Pankhurst.

undoubtedly the catalyst which originally lit the beacon of hope for a better tomorrow for all women, but it was the varied demands of the First World War, which provided women with the platform and opportunity to be able to showcase their new found plethora of skills and attributes, which largely layed the foundation of where they are today. Even politicians managed to grasp the importance of what women had achieved for their country during the war, and how beneficial their presence in a post war Great Britain, would be.

With the outbreak of the war a deal was struck between the government and the leadership of the Women's Social and Political Union, which saw all incarcerated suffragettes released from prison, as well as a sum of £2,000 paid to the movement in exchange for their support of the war and their encouragement of men to enlist in the army. To this end Emmeline and Christabel organised a rally in London, attended by an estimated 30,000 women.

Some of the organisation's members saw this as a total betrayal of everything which they collectively stood for, but the Pankhursts saw a wider picture of more jobs being available for women in the short term as well as a better tomorrow in the long term. There was the added advantage that if women showed the value of their support for the war both on the Home Front as well as on the battlefields of Europe and beyond, then there was every possibility that the time when they would finally have the right to vote, would come earlier than it otherwise might have been. It has been estimated that between 1914 and 1918, some 2 million women replaced men in the workplace, thus making those men available to serve in the armed forces.

In August 1914, men from all walks of life and from all parts of the country, left their jobs and families to go and fight. Some did it for their king and country, others did it out of honour and a heartfelt desire to do their duty, whilst there were those who saw the war as an adventure, one that saved them from a life of eternal drudgery. No matter what their reasons, the jobs they left behind still needed to be done. It was as a result of this environment that women's lives would be changed for ever.

For the first time in history women became more than wives and mothers, more than domestic servants to the rich and more than lowly paid shop workers. Almost overnight they became the very backbone of the country and throughout the war years, they literally kept the nation going. With their newfound place in the social structure of society, a whole new world was opened up. Job opportunities, which had previously been the sole domain of men, were now largely dependent on women. More women than ever before now had their own money for the first time, albeit being paid less than men for doing exactly the same job. Despite this, they were not always any better off financially, as the war brought with it many issues, food shortages being one of them, but it didn't stop there, as the lack of food stuffs, coupled with cramped living conditions, led to concerns over the health and wellbeing of the nation's children.

Women now had a freedom, many for the first time, to socialise, to make their own decisions and become an integral part of the war effort. Married women who had no other income, were entitled to a separation allowance if their husband was away fighting in the war, one of the conditions being that the wife had to stay 'faithful' to her husband. The Defence of the Realm Act 1914, actually made it an offence for a woman to pass on to a man a sexually transmitted disease, regardless of whether or not a man had given it to her in the first place.

Despite this negativity, the nation as a whole and generations of women who would follow in their footsteps, were and would be eternally grateful for a job well done in the most difficult of times.

There was a certain surreal irony attached to the deal or agreement, call it what you will, between the government and the leadership of the Women's Social and Political Union. Here was a government who had previously flatly refused to acknowledge or negotiate with the suffragettes, using the women's sometimes violent actions as an excuse not to do so, yet when it suited them, they were quick enough to strike a deal which would ultimately end up being so much more violent, in the shape of the First World War.

The National Union of Women's Suffrage Societies (NUWSS) was founded even earlier, in 1897, under the presidency of Mrs Millicent Fawcett, who retained her position until 1919. Six years later in 1925, she was made a Dame.

Unlike the WSPU, the NUWSS stood for peaceful protest and saw no benefit being gained from acts of violence. Millicent Fawcett put forward some very logical examples to further her own points. Men and women who worked, both had to pay taxes, therefore it wasn't right or fair that men had the right to vote and women did not. An even better point was the example of wealthy women who owned large houses and employed staff, but at the outbreak of the First World War, these same women still did not have the right to vote.

In 1867 she married Henry Fawcett, who was a campaigner for women's rights, and a Liberal Member of Parliament. It is an interesting point to note that on the topic of women's suffrage, more is known of and spoken about Emmeline Pankhurst and the Suffragettes than of Millicent Fawcett and the NUWSS, mainly because the latter did not draw atten-

Millicent Fawcett.

tion to itself by carrying out public acts, such as the bringing down of the king's horse, Anmer, at the 1913 Derby at Ascot on 4 June. Emily Wilding Davison stepped out of the crowd, directly into the path of the animal, an act which resulted in her death.

With the outbreak of war the focus of the NUWSS did not diminish. The organisation still campaigned for women to have the right to vote, which had always been its main purpose. Their efforts, as always remained entirely peaceful mainly due to the fact that many of their members were pacifists.

Besides being wives and mothers most, if not all women, would have had somebody close to them involved in the fighting. Despite having the constant worry of not knowing whether or not their loved ones would survive the war and return home, they had homes to look after and children to bring up.

There were officially sanctioned organisations, as well as voluntary ones, which were mainly of a nursing nature, or those that were non-combative but of a supportive role, such as driving, which still placed women close to the fighting, which to many politicians and senior military personnel, was just not acceptable.

Despite the war and its continuous need for more and more manpower for military service, the routine of everyday life back home went on as best it could. Just because there was a war on, the mechanism of normality couldn't be allowed to come to a grinding halt. What some people might, in the circumstances, perceive to be mundane and monotonous, still had to be done. This meant that what had been referred to as 'men's work' before the outbreak of war, was now in the main, women's work. Today, the role of a 'secretary' is a position which is undertaken almost exclusively by women, but before the war it was a job almost entirely carried out by men.

In the Great Britain of the early 1900s, only a quarter of women of working age, were actually employed, many in the world of domestic service, although in some parts of the country there was a long tradition of working women in mills and industries such as weaving. But on the whole, middle income married women were expected by society to stay at home and look after their husband and their children by being dutiful wives and mothers. The war changed all that. By its end nearly three quarters of women were in some kind of paid employment, although it is difficult to be totally accurate with these figures as they do not include many of the women who were employed in domestic service.

Women had become deliverers of the Royal Mail. They were taxi drivers, chimney sweeps, farm labourers, factory labour, mechanics, shop workers, men's barbers, railway guards, ticket collectors, fire fighters, bank tellers and clerks and wartime munitions workers, to name but a few. Women employed in the latter role, were affectionately referred to as munitionettes or canaries. The long hours they had to endure making shells and bullets for the war effort meant that the work was exhausting as well as being extremely dangerous. It was also a major health hazard because of components such as TNT, which they had to handle and which was the reason they were referred to as canaries as it stained the skin orange-yellow. Today's Health & Safety workers, would have undoubtedly have had a field day. It is estimated that during the course of the war some 400 munition workers died due to their almost continuous handling of TNT.

Women's willingness to undertake this work was a plus for the government of the day, as it meant that more men were available for the armed forces. After the introduction of conscription in January 1916, more women than ever before were needed in the workplace. This was a healthy situation to have during a time of war, but when it ended, there were suddenly a lot of angry and frustrated men who had been fighting for freedom and a better tomorrow, who had returned home to discover that their job was now 'owned' by a woman, with employers happy to keep them on as they were paying them less than they would a man for carrying out the same role.

There was even disagreement amongst women in relation to the workplace after the war. Some single women believed that married women and mothers should quit their jobs in deference to them and those who had been left widowed as a result of the war.

The Co-operative Women's Guild, which had been formed in 1883, by Mary Lawrenson, who was a teacher, and Alice Acland, the first editor of 'Women's Corner' in the Co-operative newspaper, had a long standing depth of support, particularly amongst those women who were of a pacifist nature. In the early years of their existence, the Guild was in the main concerned with such issues as 'home management' and the price and quality of goods for sale in the shops. With a war on, looking after a home and children was not always straightforward for women to manage. Two thirds of all food that was consumed throughout Britain was imported from other countries around the world, which became a serious problem during the war years, made worst by the German U-boat campaign of sinking all and any shipping on its way to the island nation from 1917.

It would have come as no surprise to most, especially the mothers and the home makers, that shortages of some of the most basic foodstuffs, was going to become an issue at some time during the war. Early in 1917, the

British government formed the Ministry of Food, and in the following months items such as meat, sugar and fats, were rationed in some parts of the country, mainly in and around London. Exporting food was banned and bread, a basic food item for the working classes, became so expensive, it had to be subsidised by the government and adulterated with other ingredients.

Almost everything had some kind of knock-on effect. With shortages on the food front came the drive to home grow as much as possible, such as potatoes and wheat, but with the majority of pre-war farm labourers having left Britain's fields for the trenches of the Western Front, there was a lack of farm workers available to harvest these much needed crops. It was out of such a situation that the Women's Land Army was formed in 1917 along with a government drive to encourage women to volunteer to serve in it.

The Co-operative Women's Guild supported women's suffrage and in the main campaigned for equal rights with men, as well as maternity benefits, infant welfare and a minimum wage for women.

Less than a year into the war, an International Women's Congress took place in Paris, France, its aims being to promote world peace and freedom for all nations and their people.

Women workers on the home front had not been individual to Great Britain alone. Most of the belligerent nations who were involved in the war, utilised their women folk in a similar way out of necessity.

CHAPTER TWO

MUNITIONS WORKERS

Munitions factories and the people who worked in them, were one of the most important elements of the war. It was predominantly women who carried out the extremely dangerous and arduous work to provide the munitions that the country needed to sustain the war against Germany and her allies.

Men who were not in military service and women who were not in one of the many uniformed volunteer corps, but especially the men, were always vulnerable to the allegation of being 'shirkers' or cowards, as it was naturally assumed they were not doing their duty for king and country. The wearing of an 'On War Service' badge and its engraved insignia, let people know that the wearer of the badge was involved in war work such as in munitions or in the docks. A triangular-shaped badge was issued in

Some 'more affluent' munitions workers arriving for work.

Munitions Workers Badge, 1915.   A recruitment poster for Munitions Workers.

1916 by the Ministry of Munitions solely for women engaged in urgent war work. It could give priority boarding and fare concessions on public transport, as well as indicating that there was nothing disreputable about these ladies travelling alone at night.

By the end of the war there were almost a million women employed making munitions for the British government, whereas at the beginning of the war the figure had been only just over 200,000.

Before the war there were only three government owned factories which manufactured military ordnance. These were the Royal Ordnance Factory at Woolwich, which produced both ammunition and weapons, the Royal Gunpowder Mills at Waltham Abbey, which produced cordite, and the Royal Small Arms Factory at Enfield Lock, which manufactured rifles, machine guns and other types of small arms.

By the end of the First World War there was somewhere in the region of nearly 9,000 companies and factories operating throughout the United Kingdom, which produced a variation of munitions and weaponry, but only 218 of them were official government munitions factories. Collectively they manufactured everything from, bullets, artillery shells, tanks, gas masks, ball bearings, machine guns, as well as poisonous gas. Remarkably though, when the British Expeditionary Force (BEF) left for France

"18 et 80"

Adolescence et vieillesse dans une fabrique
britannique d'obus.

A French postcard depicting British Munitions workers.

in early August 1914, the reserve stockpile for heavy artillery weapons consisted of 29 million shells, which was only sufficient for four large battles; this reflected the expectation of the War Office as to how long they thought the war was going to last. Such was the poor state of affairs in relation to munitions, in relation to who produced them and the quality of what was actually produced, that the Munitions of War Act 1915 came into being, which in turn led to the creation of the Ministry of Munitions, its initial head being the future wartime Prime Minister, David Lloyd George.

It wasn't just the potential danger from the continuous handling of some of the volatile components used in the manufacturing process, that workers had to contend with, but the ever present danger of catastrophic explosions in the factories. An estimated 400 women died as a result of these explosions and exposure to such chemicals as trinitrotoluene (TNT), nitric and sulphuric acid, whilst making and handling artillery shells. Despite these inherent and ever present dangers, being a munitions worker did provide the double advantage of better working conditions, although by no means perfect, and higher wages. It is doubtful, however, that the working conditions then would have passed today's health and safety standards.

Sadly there were numerous incidents of explosions having taken place at munitions factories during the war, many of which were not reported in the press at the time, due to government censorship. Below are a number of these incidents, and no doubt this is far from being a comprehensive list. In some of these incidents no women workers were killed but they have been included as it shows just how dangerous the job was. A staggering point from these incidents is that many of them appear very similar in how and why they took place. A logical expectation would be that the Ministry of Munitions would have been recording these incidents and passing on directives and information to the other factories under their control, in an attempt at eradicating further occurrences.

At approximately 2.00pm on 2 December 1914, with the war not even four months old, there was an explosion at the White Lee Chemical Works. The factory was a subsidiary of Henry Ellison Acid Works which manufactured picric acid and was situated in Hollinbank Lane, Heckmondwike, Yorkshire. The explosion killed ten men who worked at the factory and injured another six.

Henry Ellison's company had been employed by the government to manufacture picric acid for lyddite shells, as it had during the Second Boer War of 1899–1902. On the day in question, according to the *Spenborough*

Guardian newspaper, workers at the factory had been grinding the acid crystals into powder. Although there was no conclusive proof of exactly how the accident occurred, the Coroner, who conducted the inquest on the dead men, suggested that a spark from the grinding machine used to crush the crystals may have resulted in the explosion.

The factory was totally destroyed as were many nearby homes, with others having their windows blown out. It had only been back in operation for six weeks, having been closed for a period because of concern over safety standards. There had been a previous explosion at the same works on 20 February 1914 and a further one was to follow on 3 April 1915. This shows the pressure that was placed on munitions factories to produce their quota and the government's reluctance to close them, even if safety standards were blatantly failing.

On Sunday, 2 April 1916 there was an explosion at a gunpowder mill at Uplees near Faversham in Kent, when a massive 200 tonnes of TNT detonated. Unbelievably, the cause of the explosion had been caused when some empty sacks that had been stored near to the TNT, had inexplicably, caught fire.

Because the mill was in the middle of the North Kent marshes close to the River Thames, the explosion was heard as far away as Norwich and Great Yarmouth in Norfolk, but despite this and because of wartime censorship, the incident was not reported in the press until 29 April. No women were at the mill at the time of the explosion, as women did not work on a Sunday. Some 115 men and boys were killed, although seven of the bodies were never found, those of the other 108, were buried in a mass grave at Faversham Cemetery. The explosion at Faversham remains to this day the worst ever in the UK's explosives industry's history. It could have been so much worse as there was reportedly, a further 3,000 tonnes of TNT stored in nearby sheds which thankfully, never exploded.

Monday, 21 August 1916 saw an explosion at the Low Moor Chemical Company, near Bradford, which killed thirty-eight people and injured more than a hundred. The factory produced picric acid which was used in the manufacture of artillery shells. There were a number of explosions which rang out during the first day, which killed at least eight firemen. The factory had been situated right next to the local gas works and both buildings were destroyed by the explosions. It took three days to put out the resulting fire which damaged fifty houses which had to be demolished as they had been rendered structurally unsafe. A further 2,000 were badly damaged. Due to the wartime restrictions, the press were prevented from reporting anything about the incident.

The following is an excellent example of how the Ministry of Munitions reported explosions at munitions factories. The following article was carried in the *Dundee Courier* newspaper, dated 6 November 1916:

Munitions Factory Explosion

The Ministry of Munitions announce that a small explosion occurred at a munitions factory early on Saturday morning. One worker was killed, one seriously injured and three less seriously.

That was it, plain and simple, the basic information, without giving away the slightest indication of how or where it happened.

Barnbow Munitions Factory in Manston Lane, Leeds, or to give it its official name, the National Filling Factory No. 1, was the scene of a massive explosion on Tuesday, 5 December 1916, which resulted in the deaths of thirty-five women. The injured, of which there were many, were taken to the Leeds General Hospital.

Unlike most other munitions factories of the First World War, Barnbow was a brand new building, erected after the war had begun as the demand for more ordnance increased. Leeds Forge Company, which was at Armley, was at full capacity, producing some 10,000 shells per week. Rather than overload the Armley factory further, it was decided to build a new factory at Barnbow.

The explosion is believed to have happened when a shell was placed in a machine in preparation for having its fuse screwed into place. During the process the shell burst, as did others nearby, which set off a catastrophic explosion.

Barnbow Munitions Factory was not a lucky place as there would be two more explosions there, with death once again being the final outcome. On 21 March 1917, two women were killed and on 31 May 1918, three men were killed and another ten were injured. Ironically King George V and Queen Mary were visiting the city of Leeds at the time of the third explosion.

Barnbow highlighted the extreme pressures that munitions factories were placed under by the Ministry of Munitions to produce more and more ordnance for the war effort. Sadly, this in part led to many of these accidents. The working conditions appeared to get worse rather than better, and over time whatever inspections of these establishments were carried out, accidents kept on happening throughout the war. Perhaps the need for more and more ordnance to sustain the war effort allowed basic common sense, as well as rudimentary safety measures, to fall by the wayside or simply be ignored by unscrupulous managers and owners of some of the factories. Maybe it was simply a case of getting the job done, no matter what it took or no matter what the cost was. One way or another the government would get its shells.

On 3 January 1917 there was an explosion at the Munitions Filling Factory No. 7, at Hayes, Middlesex. At least two women were killed. The factory had begun its production on 30 October 1915, and was licensed by the Ministry of Munitions to manufacture small shells, cartridges, detonators and primers and other small items. By the end of the war, the factory, which sat on a 14-acre site, employed more than 8,000 women as well as some 1,400 men.

On Friday, 19 January 1917 at aproximately 7.00pm, there was a large explosion at a munitions factory in Silvertown, East London, which resulted in the deaths of seventy-three workers, mainly women, with a further 400 injured. So big was the blast, that some 900 surrounding homes were destroyed. The disaster occurred because of a fire in the melt-pot room, which resulted in 50 tonnes of TNT exploding, which was heard up to 100 miles away.

On 27 April 1917 an explosion took place at Cote Holme Chemical Works, in Church, which was a subsidiary of William Blythe's Chemicals. The factory produced picric, and sulphuric acid as well as TNT for use in artillery shells. It was also known locally as Canary Island, because the chemicals that the workers were constantly exposed to, especially the sulphur, turned their hair and skin, yellow in colour.

PC 819 James Hardacre, who was 34 years of age, a married man with one child, was on patrol in the area whilst local fireman, Walter Schofield, was carrying out fire safety checks on the premises. Without any warning there was a massive explosion from inside the chemical works. PC Hardacre went to investigate and on doing so found one of the magazine doors was open. He managed to close one of the doors but as he attempted to close a second, there was another explosion which killed him. Why the magazine doors were open is unclear.

The explosion was so big that nearly every window in Church was shattered in the subsequent blast. PC James Hardacre was posthumously awarded the King's Police Medal for his bravery. Six local firemen who subsequently fought the blaze and managed to put it out, were all awarded the OBE. The joint actions of PC Hardacre and the six firemen, undoubtedly saved the lives of many people that night.

Despite the scale of the explosion there was no report of the incident in any newspapers, either locally or nationally due to wartime government censorship.

The *Dundee Courier* included an article about another munitions factory explosion, on Thursday, 2 August 1917, but this time the Ministry of Munitions provided the public with more information:

Munitions Factory Explosion – Six persons killed, three injured.

The Ministry of Munitions regrets to announce that an explosion took place at a munitions factory in South Wales. Considerable damage was done to the factory, and it is regretted that up to the present the following casualties have been reported:- 6 killed, 3 injured.

On 13 June 1917 a massive explosion took place at the Hooley Hill Rubber and Chemical Works in Ashton-under-Lyne, Tameside, Manchester. The factory produced TNT for use in artillery shells. The incident took place at 4.20pm, with children already on their way home from school. Forty-six people were killed and 500 were injured. This included eight children, one of whom was killed by falling glass, whilst swimming at the local baths, and the other seven as they were simply making their way home. Nearby homes were badly damaged, resulting in the occupants being made temporarily homeless and being put up in the local school hall.

On 7 March 1918, there was an explosion at the George Kent Ltd Factory in Biscot Road, Luton. The factory, opened in 1908, manufactured both sulphuric acid and TNT. Luton newspapers did not cover the event at the time; newspapers were not encouraged to report on such incidents, as it was believed that it could both affect the morale of the civilian population as well as giving advantageous information to an enemy. According to the Luton Today website, one of the victims, May Emma Constable, who was only 22 years of age, subsequently died from her injuries in the town's Bute Hospital, some six days after the explosion occurred.

On 1 July 1918 an explosion took place at the National Shell Filling Factory at Chilwell, Nottingham, when 6 tonnes of TNT exploded, resulting in the deaths of 134 people, with a further 250 injured. So powerful was the explosion that it was only possible to positively identify thirty-two of those who had been killed. Remarkably, production at the factory re-commenced the next day.

The cause of the explosion was never fully ascertained. Despite allegations and concerns at the time, that were never proved, that it had occurred as a result of sabotage, it was more than likely down to nothing more sinister than poor safety standards, which had unintentionally become lax due to ever increasing production targets.

On a lighter side of the very dangerous occupation of being a munitions worker, during wartime Britain, some of the factories even had their own women's football teams, like Associated Equipment Company (AEC) Munitions Factory at Beckton. A photograph of the ladies team is held at the Imperial War Museum.

CHAPTER THREE

VOLUNTARY AID DETACHMENTS

As a result of previous wars in which Britain had been involved at the end of the nineteenth and the beginning of the twentieth centuries, a need had been identified for more nurses to help care for and look after soldiers who had been wounded in battle.

With increasing friction throughout Europe for many years, the fear of war was never far away, especially with the numerous military alliances that countries were making with each other, in the hope of better defending themselves against attack and invasion from a more powerful neighbour.

In 1909, five years before the war began, the War Office approached the British Red Cross, along with the Order of St John, and asked them to form an organisation of volunteers who could assist medically, in the event of war. The process was begun almost immediately and by the following year there were already some 200 Voluntary Aid Detachments, which became better known by the organisation's acronym, VADs, in place across the country, with more than 6,000 volunteer members – a truly amazing feat in such a short period of time. One of the first batch of people to join the VAD attached to Britain's Territorial Army, was Katharine Furse who went on to be recognised as the founder of the English VAD force.

Viscount Chilston, of Boughton Malherbe in Kent, was made the chief county director of the organisation across the country and liaised with the War Office. The title of Viscount Chilston had been created in 1911, for the former Conservative politician, Aretas Akers-Douglas, who had held the position of Home Secretary from 12 July 1902 until 5 December 1905, under the then Prime Minister, Arthur Balfour, making him only the second person

Viscount Chilston.

A VAD nurse.

to hold the position in the twentieth century. In 1880 he had been elected as the MP for East Kent and in 1885 he was re-elected, this time as the MP for St Augustine's which was also in Kent.

Katharine Furse was chosen to be in charge of the VAD. Along with some of her colleagues, she first went to France in September 1914. She held the position until November 1917 when she resigned, mainly as the result of an on-going dispute over the living conditions of VAD members. No sooner had she resigned as the head of the VAD, than she was offered the position as Director of the Women's Royal Navy Service (WRNS), more detailed information about which is covered elsewhere in this book.

Members of the VADs were predominantly women, but also included men. They were set up in towns and counties across the country and carried out a variety of work which allowed full time professional nurses to concentrate on the more skilled aspects of nursing. As the war continued and the casualty rates for British and Allied soldiers increased, so the demands on nurses increased dramatically, making the work which was carried out by the VADs extremely important.

A VAD section for women was made up of just twenty women, who would have to cover an entire twenty-four hour period, and in some cases cater for a large number of wounded men. Four of the section were required to be qualified cooks. Each section was overseen by a commandant who could be either a man or a woman. There was also a male or female quartermaster, who looked after the equipment, bedding and other belongings of the section, and a female superintendent who was a certified nurse and who had completed at least three years training at a hospital that had included a nurse's training school. The men's section was made up of a different configuration.

The rules and regulations which VAD members, who wished to be considered for a full time nursing post, had to adhere to, were quite strict, especially when taking into account that they were volunteers. References were required and checked before candidates were considered, and those who were accepted required a good understanding of French, as well as the willingness to work either at home or abroad. Nurses even had to provide their own uniforms.

With the war came the desire by most people to be of service in whichever way they could, and for many women joining their local VAD, was just the thing. For most it was local, which meant that they didn't have to travel too far and they could choose whether to work either part time or full time.

It was not just average members of the public who wanted to 'do their bit' during the war, some women who had a high social standing in society also wanted to be useful. For example **Vera Mary Brittain**, the well-known writer and peace campaigner, served as a VAD nurse during the First World War.

Her home address was 10 Oakwood Court, Kensington, in West London, and she worked with the London 268 Detachment. She began working as a VAD nurse on 18 September 1915 and finished her service on 28 March 1919, earning the Scarlet Efficiency Stripe, which she was awarded on 26 September 1917.

Vera worked at five different hospitals. She started her VAD career as a nurse at the Camberwell Military Hospital, which was situated in Denmark Hill. It was also known as the Maudsley Military Hospital, as well as the Maudsley Memorial Hospital. When it was requisitioned by the War Office in the early part of the war, it was used as a Neurological Clearing Hospital, for military psychiatric assessment and treatment. This was medical jargon for men who were suffering from shell shock, a psychiatric phenomenon that was new to the medical profession and affected some men who were subjected to prolonged periods of artillery bombardment, sometimes for days without any respite.

The 'thousand-yard stare' was one of the frequent and more obvious signs that a soldier was suffering from shell shock, which in itself was an ill-defined ailment. At different times and by different medical staff it was interpreted as both a physical or psychological injury, whilst others simply saw it as a man having no moral fibre.

Vera worked at Camberwell from 18 September 1915 until September 1916. From there she moved to a Military Hospital in Malta.

The Naval Hospital at Bighi, Malta.

The wounded soldier (front left) with the 'thousand-yard stare'.

Bighi Naval Hospital in Malta was widely used for the treatment of wounded soldiers from both Australian and New Zealand who had been serving during the Gallipoli campaign. By the end of the war 58,000 wounded men had received medical treatment in Malta.

Vera remained at the hospital until June 1917. Her service record then shows a two-month gap before her next appointment at an un-named military hospital, somewhere in France. She began working there on 3 August 1917 and remained until 20 April 1918. Some time after this she returned to England and on 28 September 1918, took up a post at the 5th London General Hospital that was part of St Thomas's Hospital. It had been opened for military purposes since March 1915, when 200 of its 484 available beds were set aside for military casualties.

As the war progressed, so did the need for more and more beds to cater for the ever increasing number of wounded men returning home from the fighting in France and Belgium. To satisfy this need, wooden huts were built between the existing static wards and provided an additional 302 bed spaces. By 1917 these numbers had been increased to a total of 530 beds, sixty of which were for officers and the remaining 470 for enlisted men.

As the numbers of wounded men increased so did the number of beds that were available for them, and by the end of the war, the 5th London General Hospital was able to take in a maximum of 94 wounded officers and 568 men from the other ranks.

During the four years of its existence, the 5th London General Hospital treated the injuries of 11,396 soldiers. The hospital was decommissioned and closed on 31 March 1919 and all of the wooden huts which had been added to the hospital were removed.

Vera was only at the hospital for a month. She left there on 28 October, but the same day she started work at the Millbank Military hospital, which was also in London. To be exact it was the Queen Alexandra's Military Hospital, John Islip Street, Millbank, which was situated in south-west London, but it simply became known as the Millbank Hospital. It had been officially opened by King Edward VII and Queen Alexandra in 1905, with its first patients being soldiers who had fought in the Second Boer War (1899–1902).

On the website of 'Lost Hospitals of London', the entry for the Millbank showed a couple of interesting facts. Out of those initial patients, particular consideration for treatment was given to those who had wounds that had been caused as a result of having been shot with dum-dum bullets, which were designed to expand on impact and left wounds which would not heal, those with heart and respiratory diseases, and 'those injured while over enthusiastically fighting soldiers from other regiments.'

One of the other interesting facts about the hospital was the naming of the wards. Three of the wards were named after King Edward VII, Alexandra and Princess Victoria, one was named after the Inspector General, James Barry (1795–1865), an Irish military surgeon in the British army who improved conditions for wounded soldiers. When Barry died it was discovered that he was in fact a woman, making her the first woman in Britain to have qualified to practice medicine.

During the First World War the hospital treated men with many different types of ailments. Besides the soldiers wounded by bullet and shrapnel, it also dealt with those who were suffering with frostbite, trench foot and shell shock.

Vera's last day as a VAD nurse, was 28 March 1919.

Another woman who served with a VAD, throughout nearly all the First World War, was best-selling crime writing author, **Agatha Christie**, although at the time she was just plain, unheard of Agatha Christie. She was born Agatha Mary Clarissa Miller in Torquay in 1890, and according to the 1911 Census, her home was at 'Ashfield', Bastin Road, where she lived with her mother, Clarissa, who was born in Dublin, and two servants. Her father Frederick, who died in 1901 at the age of 55, was from New York City. Agatha also had two older siblings, Margaret, who was eleven years older and by 1911 had already married and had become Mrs Watts. Her brother, Louis Montant Miller, like her father, was also born in America but became a naturalized British citizen on 11 June 1900, when he was 19 years of age.

Aged just 16, Agatha was sent by her affluent parents to Paris to study the piano. The woman who would go on to become one of the world's all-time best selling crime authors, writing novels about such characters as Hercule Poirot and Miss Marple, started work as a VAD nurse, as part of the Devon 26 section, in October 1914, after having married Archibald Christie earlier that same month. He finished the war as a lieutenant colonel in the Royal Flying Corps and Royal Artillery, although he had started the war in the Royal Field Artillery, having arrived in France on 12 August 1914, before becoming a lieutenant in the Royal Flying Corps.

Agatha Christie, was employed part time by the VAD as both a nurse and a dispenser, and from 1917 she was paid an annual wage of £17. Throughout the war she worked for a total 3,400 hours. Her first posting was at the Town Hall Red Cross Hospital in Torquay, where she worked until May 1915. After a break of some thirteen months, Agatha once again returned to working at the Town Hall Hospital, where she served from June 1916 until September 1918.

Agatha's first novel, *The Mysterious Affair at Styles*, was published in 1920. In 1926 her husband admitted he was having an affair, which led to their divorce in 1928.

A young Agatha Miller (Christie).

She went on to sell over 2 billion copies of her books, many of which went on to be adapted for films, plays and TV programmes.

Naomi Mary Margaret Mitchison (née Haldane) was born in Edinburgh in 1897 and became a notable poet, feminist and author of over ninety books.

Although she had qualified to study Science at Oxford University, with the war less than a year old and having just turned 18 years of age, she passed her nursing exams and managed to persuade her parents to allow her to enlist in the Voluntary Aid Detachment. She joined Oxford 2 VAD as Naomi Haldane and became a nursing member. In 1916 she married a barrister, Gilbert Mitchison.

Naomi Mitchison.

She went on to become a probationary nurse at St Thomas's Hospital in London in 1917. She worked part time at the Out Patients Ward at Radcliffe Infirmary in the centre of Oxford, which catered for sixty-four patients, and for six months she worked mornings at the Wingfield Convalescent Home, which was connected to the Infirmary. It only had a total of twenty beds to start with, but by 1916 wooden huts were built in the grounds which provided an additional seventy-five beds. Both of these medical facilities were part of the Third Southern General Hospital.

One of the children of wartime Prime Minister David Lloyd George, **Olwen Carey Evans** (née Lloyd George), was born in 1892. Her VAD service card showed that she enlisted in 1914 and continued her service until 1919, but above each entry there is a pencil correction which shows her date of VAD engagement was October 1915 and the date of termination of her service was in June 1916. From June to Oct 1915 she worked at the Red Cross Rest Station at Boulogne and for the last month in Hesdigneul, then at Devonshire House until June 1916.

CHAPTER FOUR

WOMEN'S ARMY AUXILIARY CORPS

The Women's Army Auxiliary Corps, or WAACs, which was a voluntary organisation, came into being in January 1917, after Lieutenant General Sir Henry Lawson, suggested to the Director of the War Office, that too many soldiers were engaged in non-military type work, mainly jobs of a clerical nature that could just as easily be undertaken by women, which in turn would release more men for front line service. The WAAC was formed to have women join their ranks to carry out these very roles, both at home in Britain and overseas in France.

Despite the organisation's title, the rank structure, although equivalent to those for men in the army, was named differently. This was mainly to distinguish the fact that the women did not have full military status. Those in charge were referred to as controllers and administrators. Below this were officials, forewomen, assistant forewomen and workers. As with similar organisations of the time, and despite its being a voluntary role, the women who chose to enrol in the ranks of the WAAC had to adhere to some very strict regulations, with certain breaches of discipline having the potential to be dealt with in a civil court of law. But despite all this, in the twenty-three months between January 1917 and November 1918, some 57,000 women served in the WAAC.

In April 1917 when Queen Mary became the commander-in-chief of the Corps, its title was changed to reflect her patronage, and became known as, Queen Mary's Army Auxiliary Corps.

Between March 1917 and February 1918, a total of 6,000 members of the WAAC were called upon to serve overseas in France. During this period only thirty-seven of them were sent home for incompetence and lack of discipline, which included twenty-one who had become pregnant as a result of 'intimate relationships' with British or Allied soldiers.

Up until the signing of Armistice, records show that a total of eighty-four members of the Queen Mary's Army Auxiliary Corps, had been killed or had died during the war, and that a further 103 had died after that time up until the end of 1921 of wounds, illness or disease. Because of the work

A recruitment poster for the WAACs.

The WAAC's recruitment in Trafalgar Square, London.

they were involved in, and the locations where they had to carry it out, they were often in dangerous situations, with most of their wartime deaths attributable to German artillery bombardments or aircraft raids, showing just how close they were to the front.

The WAAC's Chief Controller was Helen Gwynne-Vaughan, who in 1907, along with her friend, Elizabeth Garret Jackson, had formed the University of London, Women's Suffrage Society. In 1911 she married David Thomas Gwynne-Vaughan, a Professor in Botany, who died after a

Helen Gwynne-Vaughan (William Orpen, 1878–1931).

short illness on 4 September 1915, when he was the Professor of Botany at Reading University.

At the beginning of the First World War Gwynne-Vaughan joined her local VAD, but after only a matter of months, she had to quit her position to look after her husband, who was very ill at the time. After his subsequent death and a dignified period of mourning, she resumed her voluntary work.

After leaving the WAAC she was asked by Sir William Weir, the Secretary of State for Air, to take over as the Commandant of the Women's Royal Air Force (WRAF) which, like the Royal Air Force, had been formed in April 1918. It was recognised that Gwynne-Vaughan had worked wonders whilst in charge of the WRAF. It led Sir William Sefton Branckner, Master-General of RAF personnel at the time to say 'The WRAF was the best disciplined and best turned out women's organisation in the country.'

For her wartime work, Gwynne-Vaughan was made a Dame Commander of the British Empire in June 1919. She left her post in December that year.

WAACs and QMAACs Wartime Dead

Worker 31503 Mary McLachlan **Blaikley**
Worker 31673 Beatrice V. **Campbell**
Worker 15703 Margaret Selina **Caswell**
Worker 34767 Catherine **Connor**
Worker 31918 Jeanie **Grant**
Worker 15695 Anne Elizabeth **Moores**
Worker 9048 Ethel Frances Mary **Parker**
Worker 35588 Alice **Thomasson**
Worker 34864 Jeanie H.L. **Watson**
Worker 12539 Mary Minnie **Rowlands**
Member 47130 Nellie Elizabeth **Shayler**
Worker 45131 Catherine Hedley **Rodgers**
Foreworman 15646 Jane **Knox**
Worker 50182 Eleanor **Brown**
Worker 50762 Kathleen Edith Anderson **Hooper**
Worker 18847 Dorothy Annie **Reed**
Foreworman 4828 Annie Teana **Smith**
Worker 11324 Kathleen Rose **Sollis**
Worker 20110 Lizzie Dora **Stephens**
Worker 13980 Winifred Lucy **Walker**
Worker 35056 Dorothy Bateman **Maddocks**
Unit Administrator Margaret A.C. **Gibson**
Worker 44785 Rose **Cotton**

Foreworman 10732 Charlotte Mary Katherine **Simmons**
Worker 39645 Ada Elizabeth **Weller**
Worker 16451 Nellie **Whitworth**
Worker 27339 Gertrude **Mayne**
Worker 17913 Harriot **Cooper**
Worker 35272 Mrs Barbara **Henderson**
Assistant Administrator 0/1144 Marjorie Traill **Martin**
Worker 46891 Lilian Pretoria **Patrick**
Foreworman 37124 Louisa Frances **Latham**
Worker 7319 Winifred **Daw**
Worker 2732 Gertrude Winifred Allam **Dyer**
Assistant Waitress 5558 Lucy Jane **Saint**
Worker 20424 Elsie **Priestley**
Worker 20893 Gladys Annie Louisa **Bottoms**
Worker 41144 Barbara Ramsey **Todd**
Member 3812 Jemma **Wilson**
Clerk 875 Mary Edith **Harris**
Worker 50021 Helen Charlotte **Harrold**
Worker 24919 Florence Minnie **Johncock**
Worker 44400 Elsie May **Lee**

Worker 20140 Ethel **Green**
Worker 6306 May **Wylie**
Worker 50823 Elsie Uxbridge **Ing**
Worker 5648 Brunetta **Smith**
Worker 21527 Jessie **Grant**
Worker 2108 Clara **Gosling**
Forewoman 1923 Rose Mabel **Holborrow**
Worker 15323 Agnes Mary **Fransham**
Worker 9223 Alice **Twells**
Worker 11077 Emma **Howell**
Member 50290 Maude Elizabeth
  Twaddell
Worker 48257 Sheila **Dunne**
Worker 44412 Kathleen **Carroll**
Worker 16187 Ellen Graham **Thomson**
Worker 46868 Jeannie Turnbull **Wright**
Worker 10515 Doris **Quane**
Forewoman 7820 Mary Elizabeth **Smith**
Worker 20315 Jean **Roberts**
Assistant Administrator May **Westwell**
Worker 35104 Dorothy Marguerite
  Inman
Worker Lilian **Saunders**

Worker 12113 Florence Esther **Benoy**
Worker 47981 Winifred Jane **Lord**
Worker 6886 Amy Coote **Galley**
Worker 45051 Violet May **Horner**
Worker 17389 Marie Louise **Rogers**
Worker 3981 Violet Georgina **Coombes**
Worker 36023 Amy Laura **Whitcombe**
Chief Controller Violet Alice Lambton
  Long
Member 50499 Florence Caroline
  Hodgson
Forewoman 51519 Kate Swinn **Brewer**
Volunteer 18691 Agnes **McMahon**
Worker 26854 Elsie **Foulkes**
Worker 44168 Nellie **Gerrard**
Worker 48601 Jane **Bradley**
Worker 1706 Louisa **Jordan**
Worker 30438 Dorothy **Aspden**
Worker 36156 Margaret Ann **Barrow**
Worker 48452 Sarah **Billington**
Worker 47444 Susan Jane **Peake**
Worker 40785 Mary Betsy **Walsh**

WAACs and QMAACs Post War dead

Worker 2199 Beatrice Violet **Moore**
Forewoman 10037 Nellie Teresa **O'Neil**
Worker 39494 K. **Walcroft**
Forewoman 2717 Cora Cornish **Ball**
Worker 2827 Silance Ethel **Davis**
Worker 39169 Mildred Mary **Johns**
Forewoman 5220 May **Mayers**
Worker 20695 B.L. **Wills**
Worker 4624 Pattie **Hyde**
Worker 15089 V.N. **Harding**
Clerk 2615 M.E. **Matthews**
Worker 3571 K.M. **Inglis**
Forewoman 12988 F.M. **Tooby**
Worker 49651 M.F. **Brown**
Worker 33726 Alicia **Watt**
Worker 6947 Doris Mary **Luker**
Worker 47814 Mary Maria **Matthews**
Worker 1162 Blanche Amelia **Page**
Assistant Forewoman Edith H. **Routledge**
Worker 35663 Emma **Whittaker**
Member 38703 Diana Reynolds **Smith**
Forewoman 24556 Ellen Matilda **Potter**
Worker 33790 M. **Tarr**

Assistant Matron 6286 E. **Rathmell**
Worker 39581 F.H. **Mitchell**
Worker 14909 S.L. **Harris**
Worker 12310 A.E. **Scholey**
Worker 44930 Elsie May **Wright**
Unit Administrator Eleanor **Russell**
Worker 27667 Betsy **Cary**
Worker 27668 Hilda **Cary**
Forewoman 626 D.R. **Clarkson**
Worker 23193 Ethel Mary **Bailey**
Worker 45299 Dorothy Madeline
  Thornton
Worker 41900 M.M. **Chambers**
Worker 43403 M. **Johnson**
Assistant Cook 25443 Mary Ann **Evans**
Worker V. **Phillips**
Cook 14858 M. **Davis**
Assistant Waitress 21513 E.E. **Pickering**
Worker 40840 H. **Jones**
Worker 32661 A.E. **Jones**
Forewoman 7406 Maud Mary **Richardson**
Member 18716 Elsie Violet **Carpenter**
Worker 32716 Edith Ellen **Barford**

Assistant Administrator M.L. **Steibel**
Worker 48058 Esther **Ellis**
Forewoman 12180 Minnie Western **Lund**
Worker 32964 Eliza Jane **Reeves**
Worker 9936 E.B. **Hamer**
Worker 16754 Annie Winifred Mary
 Smith
Worker 47481 Edith **Natress**
Worker 51415 E. **Martin**
Forewoman 7550 M. **Bull**
Telephonist 18375 Elizabeth S. **Johnston**
Worker 1593 Winifred Mary **Steele**
Worker 10884 Annie Catherine **Miller**
Worker 42271 Winifred Edith **Absalom**
Worker 29843 Ethel Adela **Barham**
Worker 19726 J. **Last**
Worker 34544 Ivy Mary **Harland**
Member 48252 Clara **Crozier**
Worker 37102 S. **Moore**
Worker 37914 Nellie **Brannigan**
Worker 51922 B.E. **Geoghegan**
Worker 3520 J.A. **Ballantyne**
Worker 39977 W. **Matheson**
Worker 10897 Daphne Elizabeth **Powell**
Worker 51329 Jane Elizabeth **Evans**
Forewoman Clerk 49668 Marion **O'Reilly**
Worker 51688 R.A. **Corcoran**
Worker 46616 M.K. **Harrick**
Worker 52954 M. **Wright**
Worker 51457 Kate **Irwin**
Volunteer Winifred Mary **Lalor**
Worker 53144 Violet **Meal**

Forewoman 9940 Sarah Eleanor
 Maddocks
Worker 5163 F.F. **Hope**
Worker 40032 Olive Gwyndoline
 Thomas
Assistant Administrator Mary Grace
 Smyth
Worker 33956 L. **Speight**
Worker 21931 S. **Harrison**
Worker 52652 Ada **Lesser**
Worker 46829 Beatrice Trefozea **Pooley**
Worker 45491 Gladys Helen **Cobb**
Volunteer M.E. **Daly**
Volunteer 17526 M. **Wallace**
Worker 20425 Nellie Florence Ruby
 Rault
Clerk 1263 M.E.J. **Constable**
Worker 52339 Edith Gertrude **Clarkson**
Worker 17169 Catherine **Nutley**
Worker 33682 Mary **Ferguson**
Worker 6203 Florence **Gooding**
Worker 5512 Nellie May **Maunder**
Worker 3275 Evelyne Euphemia **Tait**
Assistant Administrator Anna Marjorie
 Whall
Worker 4100 Louise **Holme**
Worker 11900 Annie **Hall**
Worker 1229 F.E.M.T. **Massey**
Worker 36840 E. **Parnell**
Worker 1667 Mary Ann **Spittle**
Worker 20615 Mary Louisa **Clitheroe**
Forewoman 9341 Lena **Harrington**

CHAPTER FIVE

WOMEN'S LEGION AND OTHER FEMALE ORGANISATIONS

The Women's Legion

The Women's Legion was launched in July 1915 by the Marchioness of Londonderry, with the intention of providing a body of women who could be effectively utilised by the nation as required in a time of war, so that men could be released to go off and fight. The Legion's two main sections were cookery and motor transport. In the same month that it was formed, twenty of its cooks were sent to work at the Dartford Convalescent Hospital in Kent, with others being sent to army camps at Epsom in Surrey and Eastbourne in Sussex.

The Women's Legion went on to be so successful that during the First World War it became the largest single voluntary organisation in support of the war effort on the home front. The headquarters was at 72 Upper Berkeley Street in London with their first Commandant being Miss Christobel Ellis.

Women's Legion Badge.

Members of the Women's Legion dressed in a military style uniform even though it did not come under the control of the army, the War Office or the Government. Their work was varied and included cooking and catering for the army, as well as providing gardeners and waitresses. From 1916 they also provided drivers for motor vehicles, although this was mainly in connection with the Royal Flying Corps. They were paid a wage of 35s a week with 5d per hour paid for extra time worked.

By February 1917 the Women's Legion had several thousand cooks and waitresses, all of whom were transferred to the Women's Army Auxiliary

Corps for the remainder of the war. Despite these changes, only a month earlier the Women's Legion had advertised in *The Times* newspaper, looking for camp cooks, and motor drivers to join their ranks.

On Monday, 18 March 1918, the Women's Legion's motor drivers' section was inspected by Her Majesty the Queen at Buckingham Palace. The Legion's President, Lady Londonderry, presented the vice-presidents and headquarters committee along with other headquarters staff, the superintendents in charge of the dismounted squads, and the staff of the motor section.

A total of 160 drivers were selected to represent the Legion's total of 2,000 drivers, with four different types of vehicles that the women used. There was a dispatch rider's bike, an ambulance, a box-bodied van, a staff car and a touring car. It was organisations such as the Women's Legion that went a long way to showing the real worth of women during the war and their overall importance to the war effort.

Below are detailed other well-known women's groups of the day.

Territorial Force Nursing Service

The Territorial Nursing Service was established in 1908 as part of the Army Reforms of that year. It was the equivalent of the Queen Alexandra's Imperial Military Nursing Service, which looked after soldiers in the regular British army.

As with Territorial soldiers, the nurses were volunteers who were not paid for their service and the intention was for them to be home based, but the outbreak of the First World War changed all of that. Members were permitted to volunteer for overseas service if they were not required on the home front. Such was the shortage of qualified nurses at the start of the war, the Territorial Force Nursing Service not only welcomed married women, but if one of its members wanted to marry and remain a nurse, this was usually allowed. After the war this approach was one of all change, as fewer nurses were required, and any nurses in the service who were married had to resign.

The nurses wore a grey dress accompanied by a white apron and cap. On each corner of their distinctive cape, were metal letter 'T's'. They also wore a sterling silver medal on a red and white ribbon.

Approximately 8,000 women served with the Territorial Force Nursing Service during the war, 2,280 of whom volunteered to serve overseas. Just before the end of the war there were just over 3,000 members of the service working in hospitals throughout the United Kingdom and nearly 2,000 serving abroad.

For their wartime service, some members were awarded the 1914–1915 Star, the British War Medal, the Victory Medal and the Territorial War Medal.

The Women's Hospital Corps

The Women's Hospital Corps was formed in September 1914 by Doctor Louisa Garrett Anderson and Doctor Flora Murray. Their offer of assistance to the War Office in helping to treat wounded British soldiers, was rejected. Not to be deterred they went out to France where they ran hospitals for the French army, both in Paris and in Wimereux.

The British War Office did eventually see sense, which resulted in the Women's Hospital Corps opening up a hospital in Endell Street in London. It was unique in so far as it was staffed entirely by women, from orderlies all the way up to the chief surgeon.

The Women's Volunteer Reserve

The Women's Volunteer Reserve was formed in August 1914 by Decima Moore and the Honourable Evelina Haverfield, who had somewhat militant tendencies. The outbreak of the First World War allowed the latter the opportunity to provide women with an active role at both home and abroad.

The Honourable Evelina Haverfield.

The aims of the organisation were to form a body of women who would have a disciplined approach to their voluntary war work, which included being despatch riders, telegraphists, signallers or even trench diggers – not the most obvious forms of work that would immediately come to mind as the type suitable for a well-off woman of society.

Its members had to purchase their own uniforms, khaki in colour and military in design, which at a cost of £2, was prohibitive to most women, meaning, intentionally or otherwise, that only the more affluent tended to enrol in the organisation. Women had to be between 18 and 50 years of age to join, although older women, or those who were of the required age but not capable of such active work, were also welcomed, but offered more sedate roles such as first aid, signalling, vehicle mechanics and cooking. It had initially been named the Women's Emergency Corps and was born out of the Suffragette movement

The Women's Auxiliary Force

The Women's Auxiliary Force, formed in 1915 by Miss Waltham and Miss Sparshott, was a voluntary organisation for part time workers. What they provided was varied. They worked in hospitals, toiled as labourers on the land in the shape of allotments. They also worked in army canteens, mainly as waitresses and cleaners and also provided Social Clubs for military personnel which catered for the abled bodied as well as the wounded.

The Imperial War Museum holds photographs of the Highbury Branch of the Women's Auxiliary Force practising first aid in preparation for carrying out air raid duties.

The Women's Land Army

The Women's Land Army (WLA) was formed by Meriel Talbot in February 1917 and filled the urgent need for farm workers for the agricultural industry. It was funded and regulated by the Board of Agriculture and Fisheries.

Women, aged 18 or older, had to initially undergo four weeks of training, and by the very nature of the work, needed to be physically fit. They became affectionately known as 'land girls' and looked after livestock, including horses, sheep, pigs and cattle. They milked cows and undertook general manual labour on the farms. Their wage on initial recruitment was 18s per week, which rose to 20s a week after they had passed an efficiency test.

An estimated 25,000 young women served with the Women's Land Army between the time of its formation in 1917 to when it was disbanded in May 1919. Out of a total of 113,000 women from across all of the different female organisations, who were employed working on the land during the First World War, they made up a third of all women who carried out such work. The other groups who predominantly worked on the land, were men who came from such units as the Non-Combatants Corps, the Army Service Corps and German prisoners of war.

Women Police Volunteers

The swinging 1960s and free love were as synonymous with that period of time as Santa Claus is with Christmas, but the years of the First World War were ones based on morality, a strong belief in religion and God, as well as a desire to do one's duty in a time of need whilst controlling the devil within.

With so many towns and villages up and down the country awash with men in uniform, there was a real concern amongst the puritans of society that wanton acts of moral indecency would be carried out by young women impressed and tempted by the men in their midst, if something wasn't done to try and prevent it.

The British government had long been opposed to the idea of women police officers, but the First World War made them review their stance on the matter. Large numbers of policemen, many of whom had previously served with the Colours before the war and were on the Army Reserve, had volunteered or been conscripted into the forces. The idea of women being deployed as police officers suddenly didn't seem such a whacky idea to the politicians, especially as those who had proposed the idea, spoke in terms of unpaid volunteers. This was music to their ears and too good an offer to refuse.

The initial idea for female police was first suggested by the Head-mistresses Association. It was a theme picked up on by Margaret Damer Dawson, who at the time was the Secretary of the International Congress of Animal Protection Societies. It helped that Dawson had the support of the Metropolitan Police Commissioner, Sir Edward Henry, who was head of the Police in London between 1903 and 1918.

With Sir Edward's support, Dawson and Nina Boyle founded the Women Police Volunteers in 1914. The following year Dawson became the organisation's commandant and Mary Allen, its sub commandant. The latter appointment was extremely ironic, as Mary Allen had twice been imprisoned in Holloway for her actions as a suffragette when she was a member of the Women's Social and Political Union. During her second period of incarceration in 1909, Allen went on hunger strike and the authorities, concerned that she might die and then be portrayed as a martyr of the cause, force fed her. After her release she was awarded the suffragette's hunger strike medal.

In her book, *The Pioneer Policewoman*, Allen said: 'A sense of humour had kept me from any bitterness. I was quite as enthusiastically ready to work with and for the Police as I had been prepared, if necessary, to enter in to combat with them.'

In 1915 the Women's Police Volunteers became the Women's Police Service, and though initially their work had been focused in and around the immediate vicinity of London, their success saw them sent to other towns and cities to try and help alleviate the problems they were having.

Margaret Damer Dawson and Mary Allen had a very good relationship, both professionally and personally. Besides working with each other, they lived together quite openly in London between 1914 and 1920.

Almost as soon as the war was over, and with a new Chief Constable in post in the shape of Sir Nevil Macready, the attitude towards police women suddenly changed. The size of the Women's Police Service had risen to 357 members. Dawson and Allen decided that the time was right to ask the new Commissioner to make the women a permanent part of his force. The reason he gave for his refusal was that women were 'too

Margaret Damer Dawson (Centre) Mary Allen (to her right).

educated', a trait which he feared would 'irritate' his men. Inexcusably, Macready then went ahead and employed and trained his own female officers. Dawson and Allen had the last laugh on the matter, when both of them were awarded the Order of the British Empire (OBE).

Margaret Damer Dawson was forced to retire as commandant of the Women's Police Service due to ill health in 1920, the year in which she died. The only recipient of Dawson's will, which included her house, was Mary Allen, who replaced her good friend as commandant, but the friction with Macready was still apparent as in February 1920 he had Mary Allen and four of her colleagues charged with 'impersonating police officers' on the grounds that their uniforms were too similar to those worn by his own female officers (Metropolitan Woman Police). In fact by 1920, the Women's Police Service had been wearing the same design of uniform for six years – six years before the Metropolitan Women's Police even came in to existence. Despite this, and following a four-day trial in London, Macready and the Metropolitan Police won. This resulted in the Women's Police Service not only having to change their uniforms, but having to change their name as well, becoming the Women's Auxiliary Service.

The Women's Forage Corps

By January 1915, and with the war only six months old, an estimated 100,000 British men, who prior to the war had worked as farm labourers, had left their jobs to enlist in His Majesty's armed forces. Men, who before the war had only previously worked with hoes, spades, shovels and other farm related equipment, now had to use rifles and bayonets as their tools of work.

This left a massive void not only in manpower, but in the nation's food chain. Farmers were finding it hard to harvest their crops, which in turn meant it was becoming harder to meet the pre-war levels of food production. Something needed to be done urgently.

The Women's Forage Corps was formed by the government in 1915, and although all of its members were civilian volunteers, they came under the control of the Army Service Corps. The women's efforts were overseen by Brigadier General Sir Hill Gordon Morgan KBE CB CMG DSO. He had served during the Boer War where he was the Director of Supplies in South Africa.

At the beginning of the First World War, the army was still greatly dependent on horse power for most of its transport needs. Cavalry were still seen by most generals as the best way of engaging in mass attacks on the enemy. Horses were also used for moving artillery pieces around the

Women from the Foraging Corps.

battlefield, as well as for the movement of ammunition and other supplies, although by the end of the war such work was being carried out by motorised transport.

During 1917, the British army had some 800,000 requisitioned horses operating in the different theatres of war, all of which needed a constant supply of straw, hay and food. In the same year the Corps had 8,000 members, who wore khaki green uniforms adorned with Army Service Corps and Women's Forage Corps badges with FC shoulder flashes. In the main they were based at British depots and army camps, tasked with feeding and generally looking after the horses, but were also involved in all stages of the hay production, which included the baling, weighing as well as its carriage to the railway stations from the farms where it was harvested. It was very strenuous work, which required the women to be both physically fit and strong.

By the end of the war Britain and her Allies had used in access of a million horses and mules, yet only 60,000 of them were ever returned to these shores.

The Women's Forestry Corps

The Women's Forestry Corps played an extremely important part in the war effort. Under the guidance of the Board of Trade's timber supply department, the Corps members were responsible for the supply of wood for industry and paper production on the home front, along with timber construction in the theatres of war where British forces were deployed.

Women of the Forestry Corps at work.

The Corps included two distinct groups. One section consisted of those who had been selected to carry out the measuring and cutting of trees once they were down, whilst the others were the fellers who initially cut the trees down. Both roles required the women to be endowed with physical strength; not all of those who applied were accepted if it was felt that they would not be able to cope with the strenuous demands of the work. There was the added aspect of having to be able to handle and control the horses which were used to drag away the downed trees.

The former group usually consisted of individuals who in their everyday lives were employed in such jobs as school teachers, bank clerks or who were university graduates.

Like many of the other women's wartime organisations, members of the Women's Forestry Corps favoured a khaki-coloured uniform. It included boots, breeches, leggings, slouch hats and, to keep them cool during the warmer months, white smocks.

The Women's Royal Air Force

The Women's Royal Air Force was established in line with the Royal Air Force on 1 April 1918. Prior to this date, women who had worked with and as part of the Royal Flying Corps, were mainly drawn from the ranks of the WAACs, and those who had worked with the Royal Naval Air Service, had traditionally been drawn from the Women's Royal Naval Service.

Almeric Paget Military Massage Corps

Along with her husband Almeric, Pauline Paget had founded the Almeric Paget Massage Corps in August 1914, which in December 1915 became the Almeric Paget Military Massage Corps and in 1919, the Military Massage Corps.

Mr and Mrs Paget, were in charge of a group of fifty trained masseuses who worked with wounded soldiers. Their method of physiotherapy had proved extremely useful for the treatment of muscular wounds. Although slow in coming, Almeric finally achieved official recognition and support from the War Office and began working for the British army in France in 1917. By the end of the war, the Pagets had 2,000 physiotherapists, working for them.

Almeric Hugh Paget and his wife, Pauline Payne Paget (née Whitney), both deserve a mention at this point. Pauline was born in New York City, on 21 March 1874, and was part of the fabulously wealthy Whitney family. Her father, William C. Whitney, was many things during his lifetime, including being the United States Secretary of the Navy between 1885 and 1889.

She married Almeric Hugh Paget on 12 November 1895, she was 21 years old and he was thirteen years her senior. The ceremony took place at St Thomas's Church, New York City, one of the guests being the then American President Grover Cleveland. Almeric was quite a character having been a cowboy, an industrialist and an award winning yachtsman.

Almeric's elder brother was General Sir Arthur Paget, whose son, also Arthur, was a captain in the 11th Hussars. The family were looked after by nine servants.

In 1901 Almeric, Pauline and their 2-year-old daughter, Olive, moved to England, mainly because of Pauline's poor health, setting up home at Brandon Park House in Suffolk. Their second daughter, Dorothy, was born in 1905. Almeric became involved in politics and in 1910 became the Member of Parliament for Cambridge, serving in that position until 1917.

Some time after arriving in England, Pauline was given a large sum of money by her uncle, Colonel Oliver Hazard Payne who, during the American Civil War ,was in the Union Army. In 1863, two years into the war, he was colonel of the 124th Ohio Infantry and on 13 March 1865, was brevetted, brigadier general. After the war he made his fortune out of steel and oil, being one of the founders and original directors of the Standard Oil Company.

Shortly before her death on 22 November 1916, in Esher, Surrey, after a three-week illness, Pauline, gave each of her daughters $2 million.

Women of Pervyse

Miss Mairi Chisholm and Miss Elsie Knocker were both motorcycle enthusiasts. At the outbreak of the First World War, they both joined the Women's Emergency Corps and became despatch riders. After having being with the Corps for only a short period of time, Chisholm joined Hector Munro's intriguingly named, Flying Ambulance Corps. She then persuaded him to let Elsie join as well, pointing out that her skills included nursing, being a mechanic and that she was able to speak both French and German, attributes which would have all been extremely useful in wartime Belgium.

Elsie, Mairi and the rest of their colleagues arrived in Belgium on 25 September 1914 at Ostend. Elsie was soon to experience her first taste of the horrors and brutality of war, when she saw what turned out to be the dead bodies of twenty-six Belgian military policemen, whilst on a visit to the town of Nazareth. Each of the policemen had been shot, apparently by German soldiers, and their bodies mutilated.

Their job whilst working for the Flying Ambulance Corps, was to transport wounded Belgian soldiers from the battlefields to the nearest hospital, which sometimes could involve a very long journey. The women carried out some research and discovered that a disproportionately large number of men who had relatively minor wounds, were dying of stress during the journey as it was simply too arduous for them. They realised that what these men initially needed was a short period of rest, to recover and recuperate, not only from their own wounds, but from the trauma of what they had experienced. If this could be achieved then more of them would undoubtedly survive, and at least make it to the hospital, where they could receive the treatment that they needed.

They quit their roles with the Corps and returned home to Britain in an effort to raise funds at the end of November 1914, before returning to Belgium, where they would spend the next three and a half years. They set up 'shop' in the cellar of a bombed out house in the village of Pervyse, which they chose to name the British First Aid Post. Part of it was used as a dressing station to tend to wounded soldiers, letting them rest and providing them with hot chocolate and soup, before taking them off to the nearest hospital. They also provided hot drinks for other Belgian soldiers who were holed up in defensive positions in nearby trenches. Sometimes even these able-bodied men needed a respite from the cold and rain, which left them with coughs and colds and other similar ailments.

In January 1915, both Elsie and Mairi were awarded the Order of Leopold II Knights Cross with Palm for their courageous work which was presented by King Albert I of Belgium.

The two women became famous for their caring work in dangerous conditions, and accounts of their work started to appear in British newspapers, which in turn brought them even more attention.

Together the pair became known as 'The Madonnas of Pervyse', in the press. It wasn't just their work that brought them to prominence, it was their friendship. Even though there was twelve years between them, Elsie being born in 1884 and Mairi in 1896, they were more like sisters. Both women were awarded the Military Medal by the British authorities as well as the Order of St John. Ironically the award of the Military Medal was for rescuing a wounded German pilot in no man's land.

Although Elsie Knocker was born in Exeter, Devon on 29 June 1884, she came into the world as Elizabeth Blackall Shapter. By the age of 6,

Elsie Knocker and Mairi Chisholm.

Elsie Knocker (*Illustrated War News*, 1915).

she was already an orphan, her father having died of tuberculosis in 1890, and her mother two years earlier in 1888 when Elsie was only 4 years old. As a result of being adopted by Lewis Edward Upcott, a teacher at Marlborough College in Wiltshire, and his wife, Emily, she had a marvellous education at both St Nicholas's school in Folkestone, Kent and the Chateau Lutry, in Switzerland.

On 5 April 1906, at the age of 22, she married Leslie Duke Knocker at the Preshute Parish Church in Wiltshire. The marriage only lasted six years, and they were divorced on 23 October 1911 on the grounds of

Leslie's adultery and his cruelty towards her, which included threats and physical assaults.

During the marriage Elsie gave birth to a son, Kenneth Duke Knocker, who was born on 1 February 1907. Incredibly an entry in her record of petition for divorce dated 10 January 1911 records the following incident:

> (6). That in the month of July 1906 at Tanglin Hill, Singapore, your petitioner being at the time enceinte, the said Leslie Duke Knocker was very violent towards your petitioner, ordered her out of the house and threatened to eject her by force if she did not go, so that your petitioner being in fear of him was compelled to leave the house and she on returning took refuge with her sister in law living in the house.

At the time of the incident Elsie was two months pregnant.

Prior to having been married she had been training as a nurse at the Children's Hip Hospital in Sevenoaks, Kent. And after obtaining her divorce she attended Queen Charlotte's Hospital, which was a maternity hospital, in Hammersmith, London, to train as a midwife.

Social etiquette at the time was such that a divorced woman, no matter what the circumstances were, was frowned upon. The fact she had been beaten by her husband, would have counted for little and having a young son would not have helped her situation. It was because of society's attitude towards divorce that Elsie preferred to tell people that she was a widow, her husband having died in Java.

She married for a second time in January 1916, and this was to be a much happier liaison, and one where her social status would be much greater than it had been before. Her husband this time was a pilot with the Belgian Flying Corps, by the name of Baron Harold de T'Serclaes which briefly made Elsie a baroness. Sadly though for Elsie it would not end well; her husband Harold and the Roman Catholic Church eventually found out about Elsie's previous marriage and the deception which she had committed. Her betrayal not only resulted in the failure of the marriage, but it also cost her the cherished friendship with Mairi. The two women rarely spoke again.

The war ended for Elsie and Mairi in March 1918 when a German offensive saw them fall victim to a gas attack.

Mairi Lambert Gooden-Chisholm was born on 26 February 1896 in Nairn, Scotland. She came from a background of wealth. Her father, Captain Roderick Gooden-Chisholm, was a plantation owner in Trinidad. Her family left their native Scotland in the early 1900s and moved to Dorset. Mairi was in her late teens when her father bought her a 350cc

Mairi Chisholm (*Illustrated War News*, 1915).

Douglas motor bike, which not only did she quickly learn to ride, but mechanically she knew all about it as well, having spent many hours stripping it down and putting it back together again. It was whilst riding through the country lanes near to where she lived, that she first met Elsie.

When war broke out it was Mairi's idea for them to join the Women's Emergency Corps and work as despatch riders in London. Having arrived in Belgium, her story mostly mirrors that of Elsie, and together they became the most photographed women of the First World War. Besides the Military Medal, the Order of Leopold II, and the Order of St John of Jerusalem, she was also awarded the 1914 Star and the Order of Queen Elizabeth of Belgium.

The Women's Sick and Wounded Convoy Corps

The Women's Sick and Wounded Convoy Corps was founded by Mrs Mabel Anne St Clair Stobart in 1912, she was also a supporter of the women's suffrage movement, and took her nurses to work in Belgium, France and Serbia. She was an energetic woman who had lots of empathy for other human beings as well as a strong desire to serve and protect. Prior to this she had lived in South Africa.

Just before the German occupation of Antwerp on 9 October 1914, Mrs St Clair Stobart and members of her corps had established a hospital in the summer concert hall in the city's Rue de Harmonie, despite the risk to themselves of capture by the Germans. Some of the nurses who worked at the hospital were members of the Women's National Service League.

Mrs Mabel St Clair Stobart.

Over the course of 2 and 3 October 1915, Mrs St Clair Stobart, who held the rank of major in the Serbian army, was in command of a train which was transporting the first Serbian English Field Ambulance of the Schumadia Division, from Kragujevatz to Pirot, as the Serbian army retreated to Albania, to save itself from being overrun by the Bulgarian army. The Women's Sick and Wounded Convoy Corps consisted of doctors and nurses, but also on the train were six Ford motorised ambulances, a number of ox carts, six horses and a captured Austrian field kitchen.

By 20 November 1915 they reached the first Serbian-English hospital at Pristina, and just two days later she was part of a column which included Serbian hospital orderlies en route to Petch during the same retreat. The march lasted for eighty days, which Mrs Stobart did on horseback, over uneven terrain, the colour of her horse earning her the title of 'The Lady of the Black Horse'.

In 1916 she wrote a book entitled *The Flaming Sword: In Serbia and Elsewhere*. In the first chapter she writes:

> I am neither doctor nor a nurse, but I have occupied myself within the sphere of war for the following reasons.

After four years spent on the free veldt of the South African Transvaal, I returned to London in 1907 with my mind cleared of many prejudices. The political situation into which I found myself plunged was interesting. Both men and women were yawning themselves awake; the former after a long sleep, the latter for the first time in history. The men had been awakened by the premonitory echo of German cannons, and were, in lounge suits, beginning to look to their national defences. Women probably did not know what awakened them, but the same cannons were responsible.

Here is the amazingly long list of decorations that she was awarded for her wartime service by all of the nations which she so bravely served and helped:

- The incredibly named, Badge of a Dame of Grace of the Grand Priory in the British Realm of the Most Venerable Order of the Hospital of St John of Jerusalem;
- The 1914 Star;
- The British War Medal;
- The Victory Medal;
- The Badge and Ribbon, Order of The White Eagle of Serbia;
- The Red Cross Medal 1913, Bulgaria;
- The Medal for the Retreat to Albania (1915), Serbia;
- The Order of St Sava, Third Class (Commander);
- The Badge and Ribbon, Order of Red Cross, Serbia;
- The Medal of the Serbian Red Cross Society, London; and
- The War Medal of Serbia.

The Women's Sick and Wounded Convoy eventually amalgamated with the **The Women's National Service League** also founded by Mrs Mabel Annie St Clair Stobart along with Lady Muir McKenzie, in 1914. The Belgians were particularly happy for their assistance in a nursing capacity.

Women's National Land Service Corps

The Women's National Land Service Corps, which was the forerunner of the Women's Land Army, was formed on 6 March 1916 by Mrs Roland Wilkins, OBE. The 9th Duke of Marlborough became its president. His estate at Blenheim Palace in Woodstock, Oxfordshire, stretched for over 2,000 acres, which was used to grow crops and raise livestock.

The duke had realised for some time that with men going off to war there would not just be a need for women to take their place, but a dire necessity for them to be able to competently replace the men who had built up their skills in this area over many generations. So concerned had he been over the issue, that he raised the matter in the House of Lords in November 1915.

The following newspaper article appeared in *The Spectator* on 9 June 1916. Conscription having been brought in with the passing of The Military Service Act 1916, began on Thursday, 2 March 1916. By making even more men available for military service, it caused a vacuum of men who were able to undertake much needed and important work on the land. This in turn led to a reduction in the levels of food that were being produced.

Sir,

We are threatened in the near future with a very serious milk famine, as well as a diminution of production in our home-grown food. The men are being taken from the land in great numbers, and the only available labour on any large scale is that of women. The Women's National Land Service Corps asks all young, strong, educated women, who can give their whole time, to come and take a short training for work on the land. We want all we can get between 18 and 35, but we most particularly want those who are over 25 and have had some little experience in leading other women.

We offer a short training at 16s. a week, including maintenance, to those who can afford it, and free training to those who cannot. We also want for six weeks, from the middle of June, untrained workers for fruit picking and hay-making. Will all those who can, take their holiday then, and so help to save the home-grown food supply of the country? For further particulars apply to the Secretary, Headquarters of the W.N.L.S. Corps, 50 Upper Baker Street, London, N.W.

Those who volunteered to work for the corps, had to feed animals, milk cows and plough the fields, which meant long days and strenuous work. The women wore a buff-coloured armband, with the words 'WOMEN'S NATIONAL LAND SERVICE CORPS' printed in a reddish colour.

Queen Alexandra's Imperial Military Nursing Service

Queen Alexandra's Imperial Military Nursing Service (QAIMNS), came into being as a result of a royal warrant on 27 March 1902, two months before the end of the Second Boer War on 31 May 1902. The new service replaced both the Army Nursing Service and the Indian Nursing Service. The casualties of that war went a long way towards changing military nursing services. The British and Colonial forces lost a total of 22,000 men, but staggeringly only 6,000 of these men were killed in combat, with the remaining 16,000 men all dying of disease, a figure, that was simply unacceptable. In addition to this a further 22,828 men were wounded. Put into context, 22,000 men were killed over a period of three years. The same number of British and Colonial soldiers were killed in just one day, 1 July 1916, on the first day of the Battle of the Somme. Those wounded on the same day at the Somme, number more than the total wounded throughout the entire period of the Second Boer War.

Imagine the logistical nightmare that would have resulted from the large numbers of wounded soldiers that were brought to field hospitals, casualty clearing stations and general hospitals on that first day of the Battle of the Somme.

An estimated 10,000 nurses, both regular and reserve, served with Queen Alexandra's Imperial Nursing Service during the course of the First World War, working in such places as France, India, Italy, Palestine, Salonika, Mesopotamia and Russia. The picture was somewhat different at the outbreak of the war when there were only 300 full time members and 2,223 members of the reserve. Out of this total, 1,803 were sent abroad to work in military hospitals close to the fighting.

It is interesting to note how the criteria for QAIMNS changed as the war continued. Initially, women had to be single, aged over 25 and of a high social status in society, but by the end of the war, married women were also accepted and a woman's place in society was no longer an issue.

CHAPTER SIX

INDIVIDUAL WOMEN OF THE GREAT WAR

Dorothy Lawrence

One of the most intriguing individual stories in relation to a woman during the First World War must be that of Dorothy Lawrence, who became a soldier and served in the trenches on the Western Front.

Before looking at her military exploits, it is important to look at her early life, to see if it is possible to clear up the ambiguity of where she was born.

An article appeared in the *Daily Mail* of 24 January 2014 concerning Dorothy in which it was stated that she was born to an unmarried mother in Hendon, North London, at the end of the 1880s. It goes on to say that at the time of her mother's death, Dorothy was aged 13 or 14 and that she was then handed into the care of a churchman and brought up in one of England's cathedral cities, but it did not mention which one. This information appears to have originated from a book which Dorothy wrote, entitled *Sapper Dorothy Lawrence – The Only English Woman Soldier* which was published in 1919 and describes her First World War exploits.

Without being disrespectful to Dorothy, it would be interesting to know how much of the book is factual and how much of it is fiction to make the book more readable. Her personal involvement at the front would have been minimal, although she would have undoubtedly seen and heard things that she probably wished she had not witnessed.

There are conflicting accounts of Dorothy's birthplace on 4 October 1896 – either Hendon, Middlesex or Polesworth, Warwickshire. Her parents were Thomas Hartshorn Lawrence and Mary Jane Beddall. So if we accept as fact that Dorothy was born on 4 October 1896 and we know that when her mother, Mary, died she was 13 or 14 years of age, this would put the year of Mary's death as being somewhere around 1909.

A check of the 1901 Census shows a Dorothy Lawrence living at 12 Queen Street, Polesworth, Warwickshire. The record also shows her as being born in Polesworth about 1897. Her parents, Thomas Hartshorn and Mary Jane Lawrence, had been married on 5 November 1891 at Lapsley in Staffordshire. Mary's maiden name was Beddall, and she had a daughter, Clara, from another relationship, who was born in 1887 and who would have been four years of age when she and Thomas married. Thomas and Mary had seven children of their own: Annie, Thomas, Dorothy, Joseph, Daisy, Kitty and Isaac.

Mary died at Polesworth in 1909 which concurs with the *Daily Mail* article. Dorothy then claims she was put in care. A check on the census of 1911, two years after the death of her mother, shows her living with her father and six brothers and sisters at Calias House Farm, at Wilncote in Tamworth, where her father Thomas, was a farmer. Thomas lived to the ripe old age of 85 and died in 1950.

Both of Dorothy's brothers were old enough to have served during the war, but I was unable to establish with any degree of certainty that they actually did. Part of the problem is that with Thomas, by way of example, the British Army First World War, Medal Rolls Index Cards system, records over eighty men of that name as having served during the First World War.

If we accept that the Dorothy Lawrence who was born in Polesworth on 4 October 1896, is the one we are looking for, then there are most definitely some ambiguities surrounding the truth of how her younger years were spent. Sometimes history doesn't always allow us to have a clear picture of the past. Sometimes the best that can be achieved are the 'possibly, maybe' scenarios, based on small clues, assumptions and an interpretation of the facts as they are known; maybe the story surrounding Dorothy Lawrence comes into that category.

At the time of the First World War, Dorothy, who by then was nearly 18, was working as a reporter in London. Exactly when and why she had resolved to transform herself in to a British soldier is not known. According to Wikipedia, Dorothy wanted to be a journalist, and in particular a war correspondent. She wrote to numerous British national newspapers in an effort to achieve her goals, but to no avail. This was, after all, still a very male dominated world that she was trying to break into, it was akin to a woman trying to gain entry to one of London's gentlemen's clubs.

Having made up her mind to go it alone, sometime in 1915 Dorothy made her way across the English Channel to France where she presented herself as a freelance war correspondent. Her first attempt to get close to the front was thwarted when she was arrested by the French police who were unimpressed with her 'Press credentials'. She made her way back to Paris where she spent some time pondering what to do next. Eventually she came up with the plan to disguise herself as a British soldier.

After meeting a couple of British Tommies in a Paris café, she told them her story and drew them in to her plan. Along with the help of some of their colleagues, they collectively provided Dorothy with enough military clothing for her to dress up and pass herself off as a soldier. In her book, she refers to these men as her 'khaki accomplices'. So determined was she to succeed in her quest, she even convinced her soldier friends to teach her how to march and drill. Once she had prepared herself the best that she could, she passed herself off as Private Dennis Smith of the 1st Battalion, Leicestershire Regiment.

She set off on her journey to the front, riding on a bicycle. On the way there she met and befriended, Tommy Dunn, who was a Sapper with the 179th Tunnelling Company of the Royal Engineers. In her book she explains how every night she slept in a nearby derelict cottage in Senlis Forest, to keep the fact that she was a woman from the men she worked with during the day.

The men of the 179th Tunnelling Company were active during their period of service in the Royal Engineers. In November 1915 they were preparing to detonate a mine chamber which contained some 6,000lbs of

Dorothy Lawrence and 'Private Dennis Smith'.

explosives in the vicinity of La Boisselle in France, underneath a German held trench position, whilst the enemy were at the same time digging their own tunnel. The British mine chamber was complete by midnight on 20 November 1915, but before it could be detonated, the Germans blew their own charge which in turn set off the British charge. Six men of 179th Tunnelling Company and seven men of 10th Essex Regiment were killed.

The 179th Tunnelling Company played an important role on the first day of the Battle of the Somme when it was responsible for detonating the Lochnagar mine, which was also in the La Boisselle area, at 7.28am on 1 July 1916, two minutes before the main infantry attack began. The mine consisted of two explosions with obliterated 300–400 feet of German dug-outs, trenches as well as an entire company of German soldiers. The 300ft wide crater left behind as a result of the massive explosion, is one of the most visited sites on the Western Front today.

What Dorothy actually did during her time with the 179th Tunnelling Company, is not clear. It is highly unlikely that she would have been involved in digging any tunnels, as this was specialist work, and members of the 179th were all seasoned coal miners back in the UK, and had been specifically employed to carry out a particular role.

After spending just ten days purporting to be a soldier, Dorothy's health declined, finally resulting in her suffering fainting fits. Realising the potential situation she could find herself in if she required medical attention having passed out, she owned up and handed herself in. She was immediately arrested. Her presence caused great consternation to the military authorities, who were not quite certain what they were dealing with. Senior officers who interviewed her in both Calais and St Omer had a spectrum of what she might be, which ranged from being a German spy to a prostitute; she was even held as a prisoner of war. She was held at the Convent de Bon Pasteur and not allowed to return to the UK until after the Battle of Loos had taken place, for what security chiefs referred to as 'just in case'. Once it was realised that her reason for impersonating a soldier in France was for literary purposes, the British authorities became concerned from a security perspective, at just how easily Dorothy had breached their security and been able to walk about their trenches at will, with nobody apparently having the slightest idea that she was a woman. She was made to sign an affidavit that she would not write about her personal experiences on the understanding that if she broke its terms, the penalty would be a prison sentence.

On her return to England she attempted to write about her time in France for *The Wide World Magazine* but when the War Office heard of her intentions, they prevented her from publishing anything that included information about her exploits, invoking the Defence of the Realm Act 1914. This provided the British authorities with wide sweeping powers of restriction over the civilian population.

Some time after her return to England, Dorothy received a letter written by Sapper T. Dunn, who at the time of writing, was a patient at the Royal Berkshire Hospital in Reading, having been wounded on active service whilst in France:

Dear Miss Lawrence,

I once more take the privilege of dropping you a few lines, hoping they find you well and hearty to receive, as it leaves me to be keeping quite well at present. Well, I have not heard anything about my operation as yet, and to tell you the truth I don't want to either, as I would like to hang on till after Christmas. Well, for the moment I did not recognise you as you came down the ward the other day. You looked so different dressed as a girl from the Royal Engineer comrade-in-arms which at Albert in September 1915 you happened to be.

When I remember you I can hardly believe, though, that three years have passed since then. It seems so short time ago since you, looking so fine as a khaki soldier, joined up in our mine laying company, and spent ten days and nights within 400 yards from the Boche front line, under rifle fire, trench mortars and 'coal boxes'. Often you had to be quite alone too all through a day or night, and we never knew what intended to fall next, did we? Sometimes all sorts fell at once!

I think that a good many of the shells were aimed at the Albert Station; you know, the one that has been so much talked about. Anyhow, you and I used to get the benefit of them. I don't believe that either you or I realized till long after quite how extraordinary it was that you never happened to get knocked out. If the sergeant had not betrayed our secret you might have seen through, as a trusted soldier, the end of the first battle of Loos as well as its early stages. I can see you now stealing along that wall by midnight, ready to fall into line for night shift, and prepared with the Buff Regimental Badge as well as RE equipment.

Really as I think it over I cannot help laughing at what happened later on. You kept in a French convent until whatever news that you had gathered would have grown stale for use in English papers. Oh well, you got back to Blighty in the end.

Well, I think this is all that I will say at present, so I will conclude, with best wishes.

I remain, sincerely, Sapper T. Dunn No. 189467, RE.

For some reason, and one can only assume at Dorothy's request, Sapper Dunn's signature, has been witnessed in writing at the bottom of the letter by one of the sisters at the Royal Berkshire Hospital.

Witnessing the letter would give credence to Dorothy's story, which suggests that she thought not everybody believed it. The letter, although not dated in Dorothy's book, must have been sent sometime after September 1918 as a result of Sapper Dunn's reference to its being three years since they were comrades-in-arms in September 1915.

Although the extent of his injuries is not disclosed in the letter, Sapper Dunn appears to have survived the war as there does not appear to be a record of him having been killed.

With the war over Dorothy finally got to write an account of her time in France, although parts of it were heavily censored by the War Office. The book, entitled, *Sapper Dorothy Lawrence* was published in 1919. Although it sold well, it was not the commercial success that she hoped it would be, and her desire to have a full time writing career never materialised.

She was subsequently institutionalised in March 1925 and would remain incarcerated until her death in 1964, dying at what was then called the Friern Hospital, but which had formerly been known as the Colney Hatch Lunatic Asylum, which at its peak catered for up to 3,500 patients. One of the reasons given for her incarceration was that she had no family to look after her, but if we accept that the Dorothy Lawrence in question was the one born at Polesworth in Warwickshire, then her father Thomas and her younger brother Isaac were both still alive until 1950, and it is quite possible that some of her other siblings were as well. She was buried in a pauper's grave at the New Southgate Cemetery in Barnet.

Edith Louisa Cavell

Edith Louisa Cavell was a British nurse who was executed by the German authorities at 7.00am on 12 October 1915, for the offence of 'treason' whilst working in Schaerbeek, Belgium. Her story shocked the world once it became public knowledge, and was used by the British as a propaganda tool to get more men to enlist.

Edith was born in the Norfolk village of Swardeston, not far from the city of Norwich, on 4 December 1865. Her parents, Frederick and Louisa Sophia Cavell, had four children, Edith being the eldest. Frederick was the local vicar, a position he held for forty-five years.

Edith Louisa Cavell.

Having a 'man of the cloth' as her father, Edith's upbringing was one based on respect and care for others, especially the less well off in society. After leaving the prestigious Norwich High School for Girls, she became a governess which because of her excellent French, included working for a family in Belgium between 1890 and 1895. She returned to England, initially to look after her gravely ill father, who died the following year. She then decided on a career as a nurse and began her training at the London Hospital. Once qualified she worked at numerous hospitals up and down the country, building up her knowledge and experience, in places which were usually in less affluent areas. This included the Shoreditch Infirmary in the East End of London, where she was the assistant matron.

In October 1907 Edith was recruited by Doctor Antoine Depage to be the matron of a newly established training school in the centre of Brussels. Over the next few years her reputation as an excellent nurse and administrator continued to grow, so much so that by 1911, she was training nurses at three hospitals, twenty-four training schools, as well as thirteen kindergartens across Belgium.

By the outbreak of the war she had been living and working in Belgium for many years, but on the day Britain declared war on Germany, she was actually in Swardeston, in Norfolk, visiting her mother.

Within three months of the beginning of the war, and with German forces already occupying Brussels, Edith had started not only sheltering British and Belgium soldiers along with Belgium and French men of military age, but providing them with money and guides to enable them to reach the neighbouring country of Holland. The first two British soldiers whom she took in were from the 1st Battalion, the Cheshire Regiment – Lieutenant Colonel Dudley Coryndon Boger and Company Sergeant Major, Frank Meachin.

Boger was a career soldier and 48 years of age at the outbreak of the war. By the time the pair arrived at Edith Cavell's nursing school in

Brussels, they had changed out of their Army uniforms and into civilian clothing, to avoid detection by the Germans. Although an understandable thing to do in the circumstances, they would have both clearly understood the potential ramifications of their actions. If discovered in civilian clothes they ran the real risk of been shot as spies. The risks for Edith were even greater because when the Germans entered Brussels on 20 August 1914, her nurses' training school became a Red Cross hospital where she started caring for more and more German soldiers. The surprising point here is that the Germans allowed a foreign national from an enemy nation to continue in her position as the hospital's matron. Despite treating so many German soldiers as well as being continually supervised by them, by early 1915 she had some 200 English, French and Belgian soldiers in her nursing school.

Edith was arrested by Otto Mayer of the German Secret Police on 6 August 1915. She was court martialed, her trial lasting for two days. She was found guilty, with the main evidence against her being her own admission, and sentenced to death by firing squad. She then spent ten weeks incarcerated at the Saint-Gilles prison in Brussels before her execution was carried out at dawn on 12 October 1915 at the country's National Shooting Range at Schaerbeek on the outskirts of the Belgium capital. Twenty-seven people had been arrested by the Germans in relation to assisting British, Belgian and French soldiers escape, five of whom, including Edith Cavell, were sentenced to death, although in the end only Cavell and one other, Philippe Baucq, were executed.

Edith Cavell's cell at St Gilles Prison in Brussels.

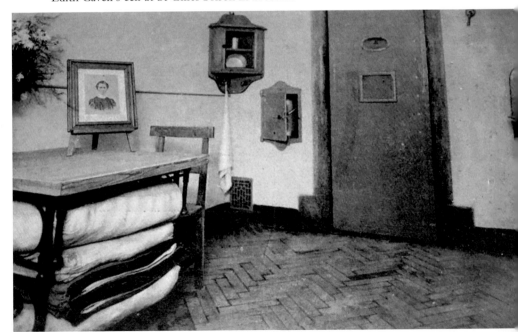

A postcard depiction of Edith Cavell's execution.

Despite pleas for mercy from many countries, including America, which had not yet entered the war, the executions still went ahead, even though there was disagreement amongst some German figures as to what should be done with her. Although on the international stage Edith Cavell's death was met with disbelief, shock and horror, Germany, by the letter of the law, had acted correctly. But her execution by firing squad was fully exploited by the British authorities, who used it to encourage men to enlist in the army.

The propaganda machine did not stop there as different accounts of her execution were proffered in an attempt at raising anti-German feelings amongst the British people and her allies. One such story claimed she had a heart attack immediately before her execution was carried out and whilst lying unconscious on the ground, the German officer in charge of the firing squad shot her dead with his revolver. Another account was that one of the German soldiers, who were part of the firing squad, refused to fire on Edith Cavell and was also shot dead by the same German officer.

In the following picture postcard of Edith Cavell's grave in Brussels, the man with the walking stick standing immediately to the left of the grave appears to be in the uniform of a member of the Royal Flying Corps or Royal Air Force, either way, it was a photograph either very late in the war or soon after the signing of the Armistice. After the war Edith's remains were exhumed and brought back to England. A memorial service took

Postcard showing Edith Cavell's grave in Brussels.

place at Westminster Abbey on 19 May 1919, which was attended by King George V. After the service Edith's body was then transported by train to Norwich where it was re-buried in the grounds of Norwich Cathedral.

A footnote to Edith Cavell's death was that of Georges Gaston Quien. An article in the *New York Times* newspaper dated 6 September 1919:

CAVELL BETRAYER CONDEMNED TO DIE
Georges Gaston Quien Convicted by French Court Martial of Treasonable Dealings.

Paris Sept 5 – Georges Gaston Quien, on trial before a court martial charged with having had treasonable dealings with the Germans and with having betrayed Edith Cavell to them, was today convicted and condemned to death.

Georges Gaston Quien, who when the war began was serving a jail sentence in St Quentin in connection with espionage case unearthed at Versailles in 1913, was liberated by the Germans when they took the town.

He was arrested early in 1919 by the French authorities, who charged that after his release from St Quentin he went to Prince and Princess Croy in Belgium and later denounced them to the German officials of occupation as having aided French prisoners of war to escape. The Princess, in consequence, was condemned to ten years imprisonment at hard labor.

The Memorial to Edith Cavell in Brussels.

Memorials to Edith Cavell Statue – St Martins Place, London (*left*) and Norwich (*right*).

Quien is said to have gone afterward to Brussels, where he went into the hospital service of Edith Cavell, the English nurse. The indictment against him charged that after having obtained funds and help from Miss Cavell, Quien went to Holland, returned to Brussels as a German agent and betrayed Miss Cavell to the German commandant. Quien denied all these charges at his trial.

In the taking of evidence, other women testified that Quien had betrayed them to the Germans. Quien was brought to trial on Aug. 25.

Quien had gone to Edith Cavell purporting to be a French soldier who needed safe passage out of the country, the reality was he was simply gaining as much evidence against her and her co-conspirators as he could, which subsequently led to Edith Cavell's arrest and execution.

Gabrielle Petit

Gabrielle Alina Eugenia Maria Petit was born in Tournai, Belgium on 20 February 1893. Her mother died when she was quite young and her father sent her to a Catholic boarding school in nearby Brugelette.

Gabrielle Petit.

Like most young people she wanted excitement in her life, and the attraction of the hustle and bustle of a city life drew her to Brussels where she was working as a shop worker at the outbreak of the First World War. She joined the Belgium Red Cross and, after only a short period of time, she helped her fiancé, Maurice Gobert, a Belgian soldier, escape across the border to Holland. She and Maurice had first met in 1912. Maurice had been in the Belgium army before the war and was in the thick of the fighting as soon as Germany had invaded. He was wounded sometime during the four-day Battle of Hofstade, at the end of September 1914, where he was captured by the Germans. But Maurice was a determined young man and for him the war was not over. He managed to escape from his captors and made his way home to his parents who lived in the town of Fontaine l'Eveque.

As a result of the journey to and from the Dutch border Gabrielle picked up some useful information about German troop locations and

NUMÉRO 30   JUIN 1915

PRIX DU NUMÉRO — élastique, de zéro à l'infini (prière aux revendeurs de ne pas dépasser cette limite)

LA LIBRE BELGIQUE

Acceptons previsoirement les sacrifices qui nous sont imposés......
et attendons patiemment l'heure de la réparation.
Le Bourgmestre
ADOLPHE MAX.

FONDÉE
LE 1ᵉʳ FÉVRIER 1915

Envers ce personnes qui dominent par la force militaire notre pays,
ayons les égards que commande l'intérêt général. Respectons les
règlements qu'elles nous imposent aussi longtemps qu'ils ne portent
atteinte ni à la liberté de nos consciences chrétiennes ni à notre
Dignité Patriotique.
Mgr MERCIER.

BULLETIN DE PROPAGANDE PATRIOTIQUE — RÉGULIÈREMENT IRRÉGULIER
NE SE SOUMETTANT A AUCUNE CENSURE

| ADRESSE TÉLÉGRAPHIQUE ·

KOMMANDANTUR - BRUXELLES | BUREAUX ET ADMINISTRATION
ne pouvant être un emplacement
de tout repos, ils sont installés
dans une cave automobile | ANNONCES : Les affaires étant nulles
sous la domination allemande, nous
avons supprimé la page d'annonces et
conseillons à nos clients de réserver
leur argent pour des temps meilleurs. |

AVIS.

On nous fait à nouveau l'honneur de s'occuper de notre modeste bulletin. Nous en sommes flattés, mais nous nous voyons, forcés de répéter ce que nous avons déjà dit pour notre défense. Ce n'est certes pas nous qu'on peut accuser sans manquer à la vérité, de provoquer nos concitoyens à la révolte. Nous ne manquons pas une occasion de precher la patience, l'endurance, le calme et le respect des lois de la guerre. Aussi profitons-nous de cette occasion qui nous est offerte pour répéter l'avis que nous avons déjà inséré :

RESTONS CALMES !!!

Le jour viendra (lentement mais surement) ou nos ennemis contraints de reculer devant les Alliés, devront abandonner notre capitale.

Souvenons-nous alors des avis nombreux qui ont été donnés aux civils par le Gouvernement et par notre bourgmestre

SON EXCELLENCE LE GOUVERNEUR Bⁿ VON BISSING ET SON AMIE INTIME

NOTRE CHER GOUVERNEUR, ÉCŒURÉ PAR LA LECTURE
DES MENSONGES DES JOURNAUX CENSURÉS, CHERCHE LA VÉRITÉ
DANS LA « LIBRE BELGIQUE »

M. Max : SOYONS CALMES !!!

Faisons taire les sentiments de légitime colère qui fermentent en nos cœurs.

Soyons, comme nous l'avons été jusqu'ici, respectueux des lois de la guerre. C'est ainsi que nous continuerons à mériter l'estime et l'admiration de tous les peuples civilisés.

Ce serait une INUTILE LACHETÉ, une lacheté indigne des Belges que de chercher à se venger ailleurs que sur le champ de bataille. Ce serait de plus EXPOSER DES INNOCENTS à des représailles terribles de la part d'ennemis sans pitié et sans justice.

Méfions-nous des agents provocateurs allemands qui, en exaltant notre patriotisme, nous pousseraient à commettre des excès.

RESTONS MAITRES DE NOUS-MÊMES ET PRÊCHONS LE CALME AUTOUR DE NOUS. C'EST LE PLUS GRAND SERVICE QUE NOUS PUISSIONS RENDRE A NOTRE CHÈRE PATRIE.

L'ORDRE SOCIAL TOUT ENTIER DEFENDU PAR LA BELGIQUE.

Le 3 août, le Gouvernement allemand remet à la Belgique une note demandant le libre passage pour ses armées sur son territoire, moyennant quoi l'Allemagne s'engage à maintenir l'intégrité du royaume et de ses possessions, Sinon, la Belgique sera traitée en ennemie. Le roi Albert a douze heures pour répondre. Devant cet ultimatum, il n'hésite pas. Il sait que l'armée allemande est une force terrible. Il connait l'empe-

reur allemand. Il sait que l'orgueilleux, après une telle démarche, ne reculera plus. Son trône est en jeu, plus que son trône . les sept millions d'âmes — quelle éloquence prennent les vulgaires termes des statistiques dans certaines circonstances! — qui lui sont confiées . il voit en esprit ce beau pays indéfendable ces charbonnages, ces carrières, ces usines, ces filatures, ces ports, cette florissante industrie épanouie dans ces plaines ouvertes qu'il ne pourra pas préserver. Mais il s'agit d'un traité où il y a sa signature. Répondre oui à l'Allemagne, c'est trahir ses consignataires, le

PRIÈRE DE FAIRE CIRCULER CE BULLETIN

La Libre Belgique **newspaper.**

movements which on her return to Brussels, she passed on to British Intelligence. Suitably impressed, they asked her to work for them in Belgium by recording details of German troop movements. After a brief period of training in England, she returned to her country to begin her work.

The Belgium newspaper, *Le Patriot*, which had been founded in 1884 by brothers, Victor and Louis Jourdain, was renamed at the beginning of the war, when it became *La Libre Belgique* and part of the country's wartime underground press.

Gabrielle became involved in clandestinely delivering copies of the newspaper around the city, as well as the underground mail service, *Mot du Soldat* which was much more precarious than it might at first sound. She was eventually betrayed by a German who had passed himself off as a Dutchman, and was arrested and held at the St Gilles Prison in February 1916. Her trial did not take place for more than a year, when she was found guilty and sentenced to death on charges of spying. Despite the best attempts of the German authorities to get Gabrielle to divulge the names of her fellow agents, which included offering her amnesty, she was executed by firing squad on 1 April 1916 in Schaerbeek.

Memorial to Gabrielle Petit in Brussels.

It was not until after the war that her exploits were fully acknowledged and appreciated, when she became a Belgian heroine. A statue of her was erected in Place Saint-Jean in Brussels. Following the signing of the Armistice, Gabrielle was given a state funeral in Brussels, which was attended by large crowds of people, including the Belgian Queen Elizabeth, the Prime Minister, Leon Delacroix and Cardinal Mercier of Brussels.

It is quite astounding when comparing the circumstances surrounding Gabrielle Petit with Edith Cavell. The execution of the latter caused worldwide shock and disbelief, and rightly so. Gabrielle Petit's execution by the Germans took place at the exact same location and was only six months after Cavell's, but it hardly received a mention and certainly did not stir the emotions in the same way Edith Cavell's execution had.

Sarah Aaronsohn

Sarah Aaronsohn was part of a Jewish spy ring and worked for the British during the First World War. She was born on 5 January 1890 to Romanian immigrants from Baku, Efraim and Malka Aaronsohn in Zichron Yaakon, Israel, which was then part of the Ottoman Empire. It was also where she would die at the relatively young age of 27.

Sarah was an intelligent and determined woman who could speak at least six languages, including Hebrew, French and English. She was married to a wealthy man from Bulgaria, but in December 1915 when the marriage failed, she left and returned home.

Sarah Aaronsohn.

One of the main questions which always comes to mind in relation to this topic, is why do people decide to become spies? There is no one reason for this, but it is certainly an extremely dangerous occupation no matter whether it is carried out by men or women. Constantly on edge, not knowing who they can or cannot trust, wondering if somebody is going to betray them. On many occasions even their families know nothing of what they are doing.

What in historical terms is referred to as the 'Armenian Genocide' began on 24 April 1915 and continued up to and after the end of the First World War. It was an attempt by the Turkish led Ottoman Empire to systematically exterminate those subjects within its own borders who were Armenian. The estimates of those murdered, varies from between 800,000 and 1.5 million. Armenians were deported, subjected to forced labour, sent on death marches and starved of food and drink. One hundred years on, Turkey, the successor to the Ottoman Empire, still refuses to describe these killings as genocide, stating that it is not 'an accurate term for the mass killings of Armenians that began under Ottoman rule in 1915.'

In the case of Sarah Aaronsohn it was because she had witnessed at first hand some of the murders carried out by the Ottoman Empire against the Armenians, which convinced her to spy for the British. She was a member of the Netzach Yisrael Lo Ishaker (Nili), which in English means 'The Eternal One of Israel does not deceive'. The group's main aim was to free Palestinian Jews from the oppression of Turkish rule. This was a family affair, with the leaders of the organisation being Sarah, her sister Rivka, her two brothers Aaron and Alexander, along with Rivka's fiancé Avshalom Feinberg. The group had about forty spies who were constantly gleaning information about Ottoman troop movements and other relevant information and passing it on to the British. Alexander actually served with the Turkish army during part of the First World War.

A carrier pigeon was to be Sarah's ultimate undoing in September 1917. She had attached a message to it and sent it on its way to the British authorities. Unfortunately for Sarah, it was intercepted by the Ottoman Turks and the message was deciphered. The following month saw her and other members of the group arrested. Sarah and her father were both tortured by their captors, Sarah for a total of four days, but still she did not provide her captors with any useful information about the organisation or any of its members.

The decision was then taken to transfer her to Damascus for further torture. The fact that she was tortured for so long, strongly suggests that the Ottomans had little or no actual evidence against Sarah, because if they had then there would have been no reason to torture her for so long, they could have simply put her before a court martial. Amazingly when Sarah asked to be allowed home to change her blood-stained clothes, her request was granted. She had made the request because she no doubt knew what was waiting for her in Damascus, more torture which would possibly lead to her death.

Scott Anderson's book entitled *Lawrence in Arabia* states that, 'she managed to shoot and kill herself with a pistol concealed under a tile in the bathroom. Sarah shot herself in the mouth on Friday, 5 October 1917. Even this did not end her torment. While the bullet destroyed her mouth and severed her spinal cord, it missed her brain. For four days she lingered in agony.'

It would be fair to assume that Sarah took her own life not out of any personal fear, but because she had guessed that the torture she was soon to endure in Damascus was going to become extreme, brutal and severe, and she wanted to make absolutely certain that she did not name or implicate any of her friends or other family members. In sacrificing her own life, she undoubtedly saved the lives of others.

The following passage is taken from the book, *A Spy for Freedom*, which was written by Ida Cowen and Irene Gunther and was first published in 1984:

Tears welled in the prisoner's eyes as she turned and threw a long backward glance down the street. The soldier in the lead removed her rope and chain, then pushed her aside so he could lead the way in to the house.

Anger flashed in her blue eyes. 'This is my home. Surely I am allowed to wash my wounds and change my clothes in privacy. You would not deny a woman that privilege?'

Abashed, he stood back and let her pass. The soldier's eyes followed her as she hobbled down the garden path. When she disappeared into a small building on the left of the main house, they stood at ease, their rifles resting on the ground. One man pulled out a pack of cigarettes and passed it round. The sound of running water came from an open window.

Inside the woman pressed a button on the wall to release a secret panel, then reached in her hand and pulled out a revolver. In the bathroom the water continued to run. As she reached the safety catch, a loud knocking came on the door.

'Hurry up, or we'll come in and get you!'

'I'm almost ready, just one more minute.'

She raised the revolver to her mouth, then hesitated. Did she have the courage to take her own life? Did she have the right? But what else could she do? Today the Turks would take her to their main prison in Nazareth, where the torture would begin again, the whiplashes on the soles of her feet, the boiling hot eggs under her armpits, the pincers tearing her flesh to shreds.

They'd tortured her for three days, and she'd told them nothing; but now her strength was draining away. If the pain began again, she was afraid she would break down and reveal the names of her comrades, and send them all to their deaths.

The knocking on the door began again. Again she raised the revolver. Her quivering mouth opened to receive it. 'Oh, God, let the British come soon and deliver my people Sh'ma Israel.'

A single shot rang out.

Ramming the door in with the butts of their rifles, the Turkish guards stormed into the house. Their prisoner lay sprawled on her back on the floor, blood pouring from her mouth. The revolver was still clutched in her hand.

The fact that she had planned to take her own life to save her friends shows her real strength and bravery. Her home is now a museum and young children are taught about her at school.

Sarah Aaronsohn died on 9 October 1917. Her death threw up another issue in relation to her funeral as Jewish views on suicide vary, but in essence suicide is forbidden in Jewish law, and in previous times it was considered to be a sin. Initially Sarah was forbidden a traditional Jewish funeral and burial in a Jewish cemetery, but denying such a solemn occasion to a wartime heroine, would have been an extremely unpopular course of action. It is unknown if anybody ever complained about Sarah's burial in the local cemetery, I somehow doubt it. Sarah was buried next to her mother's grave in her home town cemetery in Zikhron. This came about due to a large dose of common sense and a compromise. A small ornate metal fence was erected around the graves of Sarah and her mother, which was a subtle and symbolic way of removing her grave from the rest of the cemetery's hallowed ground.

Gertrude Bell

Gertrude Bell was an extremely unusual woman for her day. She was, over a period of years, a writer, traveller, political officer, archaeologist, explorer, photographer, cartographer and, during the First World War, a spy for the British authorities.

Gertrude Margaret Lowthian Bell.

She was born in Washington Hall, County Durham on 14 July 1868, to parents Sir Hugh and Mary Bell, who three years later died giving birth to a son. As she grew up, Gertrude was able to indulge her passion for travel and exploration, mainly due to her family's wealth.

She had attended Lady Margaret Hall College at Oxford University for two years, where she acquired a First Class Honours Degree in Modern History. Gertrude was a linguist of some renown, able to speak German, French, Persian, Japanese and Arabic. All of her different attributes, including personal contacts and knowledge of the Middle East, made her an extremely valuable asset for British Intelligence. She could get to people and places that simply would not be available to nearly anybody else. Even as a women in an extremely male-dominated environment, which the Middle East was at the time, she was a very well respected individual. However, as a white woman with red hair, she must have drawn attention wherever she went.

With the war into its second year, Bell was summonsed to Cairo and assigned to the Army Intelligence Headquarters there, beginning her work in November 1915. Initially her contribution was to process her own information, and that of others, on the topic of Arab tribes, to see which would be likely to fight alongside the British, against troops of the Ottoman Empire. On 3 March 1916, Gertrude was sent to assist the British army in Basra, where she set about drawing detailed maps of the country for military purposes.

Like Sarah Aaronsohn, Gertrude also witnessed at first hand the shocking images of the Armenian Genocide. An intelligence report that she submitted contained the following information that painted a definitive picture of how the Armenian population were systematically being brutally murdered:

> The battalion left Aleppo on 3 February and reached Ras al-Ain in twelve hours. Some 12,000 Armenians were concentrated under the guardianship of some 100 Kurds. These Kurds were called gendarmes, but in reality were mere butchers; bands of them were publicly ordered to take parties of Armenians, of both sexes, to various destinations, but had secret instructions to destroy the males, children and old women. One of these gendarmes confessed to killing 100 Armenian men himself. The empty desert cisterns and caves were also filled with corpses. No man can ever think of a woman's body except as a matter of horror, instead of attraction, after Ras al-Ain.

Bell carried on her work throughout the war, receiving the Order of the British Empire in 1917, and remained in service after the signing of the Armistice. She was, in part, one of those responsible for the post war reshaping of the Middle East, which came out of the Cairo Conference in 1921, and which Bell attended.

Her health had been an issue for a few years before her death. She had bronchitis, made worse no doubt, by her heavy smoking, and in 1925 she developed pleurisy. Gertrude Bell was found dead on 12 July 1926 in Baghdad from an apparent overdose of sleeping tablets, which will always leave the unanswerable question, of whether her death was a suicide or an unfortunate accident.

Her funeral took place at the British Cemetery in Baghdad and was well attended, by her friends, colleagues and the newly appointed King of Iraq,

King Faisal. The Prime Minister and members of the Cabinet, Sir Henry Dobbs, the High Commissioner, Air Vice Marshal Sir John Higgins, a number of Sheiks and the British and Iraqi officers who were advisers to the Army of Iraq. Troops lined the entire route of the cortege, with massive crowds out on the streets to pay their last respects, to a much loved and much respected woman.

Louise de Bettignies

Louise Marie Jeanne Henrietta De Bettignies was born on 15 July 1880. She was a French woman who spied for the British during the First World War, using the pseudonym of Alice Dubois.

She was an intelligent girl and well educated at both the Sister of the Sacred Hearts in Valenciennes and with the Ursuline religious order at three different locations throughout the south-east of England. She continued her studies in England for five years between 1898 and the 1903, and only returned home when her father died at the family home in the French city of Lille.

Once back in Lille she attended the city's university, from where she graduated in 1906. She spent the next eight years working as a personal tutor, mainly to children of Royal families throughout Europe, including Princess Elvira of Bavaria in Austro-Hungary. Whilst there, she was offered a similar position to tutor the children of Ferdinand Joseph, the heir to the Austrian throne, but she declined the offer and returned to France.

Louise lived with her sister Germaine, whose husband, Maurice Houzet, had been mobilised with the French army, at their parent's home at 166 Rue d'lsly, in Lille.

Louise de Bettignies.

There had been confusion and disagreement about how best to deal with the imminent threat from German forces. The city had been inhabited as far back as 2000 BC, with the foundations of the modern city originating from around 640 in the seventh century. A consequence of this long and colourful history was that the city had its fair share of historic buildings, which was possibly behind the decision to declare Lille as an 'open city' – not a unanimous decision by any means.

A small force of less than 3,000 men of the French Cavalry Corps, led by Commander Conneau, was despatched to Lille for its defence. The German soldiers surrounding the city, were a much larger force and better equipped. Without a care for historic sentiment, the Germans unleashed a sustained and ferocious artillery assault on the city's small band of brave defenders, destroying more than 2,000 buildings in the process.

Louise de Bettignies was 28 years of age at the outbreak of the war, and seeing at first hand the devastation that it caused had left a lasting effect. She helped the best way she could during the fighting by delivering ammunition to the Belgian soldiers, and writing letters to the families of dying soldiers from both sides in the makeshift hospitals which sprang up to cater for a never ending stream of wounded soldiers.

The German bombardment lasted from 4 to 13 October 1914, before they took the city. Louise was saddened by the loss of her city to the Germans, so much so that she was moved to do something about it. She first came to the attention of the British Secret Service when she arrived by boat at Folkestone on her way to unoccupied France, where she was going to be with her parents. Her ability to speak and understand English was immediately picked up on, but she refused approaches by the British to become one of their spies. A short time later she was approached by the head of the French Secret Service on behalf of the British and agreed to their request. Her code name was Alice Dubois. After some initial training in London she returned to Lille, where she met up with Leonie Vanhoutte from Roubaix who had already assisted a number of Allied soldiers escape from the Germans.

Amazingly she ran her own spy network of over a hundred people from her home in Lille, which helped provide the British with some invaluable information concerning German movements throughout northern France. In the nine months, between January and September 1915, when the group was in operation, it has been estimated that it saved the lives of a thousand British soldiers. So impressed were her British spy masters that they gave her the nickname of 'the queen of spies'. A book was written and published about her exploits in 1935, by Major Thomas Coulson, carrying the same title.

In late 1915 her network managed to discover information concerning the preparation of a large impending attack by the Germans at Verdun, due to take place sometime in early 1916. This information was passed on to the British authorities, who in turn passed it on to the French, who refused to believe it. The Battle of Verdun began on 21 February 1916 and finished on 20 December the same year, lasting nearly ten months. French casualties for the battle are estimated to have been between 315,000 and 542,000 men, of which an estimated 160,000 were killed.

Leonie Vanhoutte was arrested in early September 1915 and in an unrelated incident, Louise Bettignies was arrested by the Germans after having being stopped by them at Foyennes in Belgium. Initially the connection between the two women was not made, but it came to light eventually. At their subsequent trial in Brussels, on 16 March 1916, Leonie was sentenced to fifteen years in a penal colony, whilst Louise was sentenced to death, which was then commuted to life imprisonment with forced labour, harsh even for a man.

Having been in captivity for two and a half years at the Siegburg penal institution she developed pleural abscesses, which were poorly operated on at St Mary's Hospital in Cologne. After having being admitted to hospital in Cologne on 28 July, she died on 27 September 1918 and was buried in Cologne.

Her body was not repatriated to France until 21 February 1920, due in large part to all of the upheaval of the war and its immediate aftermath. She was reburied in the cemetery at Saint-Amand-les-Eaux. After her death came the true recognition of her existence and the many lives that she had helped to save. The British awarded her the Military Medal and the Order of the British Empire and France recognised one of her own heroines with the Croix of the Legion of Honour and the Croix de Guerre 1914–1918 with palms.

Marthe Mathilde Cnockaert

Marthe Mathilde Cnockaert was born on 28 October 1892 in the village of Westrozebeke in Belgium. She had decided on a life in the medical profession and following her dream, she attended Ghent University to train as a nurse. When the war came along, Marthe was still only 22 years of age and broke off her studies and volunteered to work as a nurse in a German hospital that was situated in her village, helping to treat wounded soldiers. Her skills as a nurse and her ability to speak French, English, German and Flemish, made her a very respected member of the hospital staff, so much so that the Germans awarded her the Iron Cross for her nursing service.

In 1915, with Westrozebeke becoming too dangerous a location to treat the wounded soldiers, the hospital was moved to Roeslare, or in French, Roulers, a railway hub and the town where her parents had relocated after their home had been destroyed in Westrozebeke.

Soon after her arrival in Roulers, Marthe was approached by an old family friend and a former neighbour, Lucelle Deldonck, who told her that she was a member of the British Intelligence Service and wished to recruit her to become part of the network which operated out of Roulers. That conversation must have been an anxious moment for Marthe, as although she knew Lucelle, she could not have known whether or not she was being set up to try and find out where her true allegiance lay. It was a genuine approach, however, and Marthe readily agreed to become part of the spy network, whose members were other Belgium women. Her code-name was 'Laura'.

Not only did she work as a nurse at a German hospital, but also as a waitress at her parent's café, which gave her every opportunity to pick up some useful information and intelligence which she could then pass on to the British.

Ironically, Marthe was also approached by an agent of the German Intelligence Service who was billeted in her home. He tried to recruit her to work for the Germans and so for a while she worked as a double agent. This arrangement eventually became too dangerous and, not wanting her German handlers to discover her secret and where her real allegiance lay, she arranged for the German agent, who in effect was her handler, to be killed.

By chance Marthe discovered a disused sewer tunnel system, which ran under a large German ammunition dump. She decided to place an explosive charge in the sewer in an attempt to blow up the German munitions. Unfortunately, whilst she was planting the explosives, Marthe lost her watch, which she wasn't aware of at the time. The watch, engraved with her initials, was subsequently found at the scene and once it was discovered who it belonged to, Marthe was arrested. At her trial in November 1916, she was found guilty and sentenced to death, but due to her expertise as a nurse and the fact that she had been nursing German wounded, for which she had received the Iron Cross, the sentence was commuted and Marthe spent two years in prison in Ghent, finally being released from German custody by British troops, just after the signing of the Armistice.

Had she not been a holder of the Iron Cross she would have undoubtedly been executed for a crime of that magnitude. After the war, Marthe was rightly recognised for her wartime work by the British, Belgian and French governments. She was made a member of both the French and Belgian Legions of Honour, awarded a certificate for gallantry by Winston Churchill and was Mentioned in Despatches by Field Marshal Sir Douglas Haig on 8 November 1918 in recognition of the information which she supplied to British Intelligence during the war.

After the war she married a British Army Officer, John 'Jock' McKenna and turned her hand to writing. Her first book, entitled *I Was a Spy*, which was her memoir, was published in 1932. It went on to become a film, with the same title, in 1933. Over the next nineteen years, a further sixteen novels followed, the last of which, *What's Past is Prologue*, was published in 1951, the year Marthe and John were divorced.

Marthe died in Westrozebeke, the Flanders village where she was born, on 8 January 1966. She was 73 years of age.

There were undoubtedly other female spies in the pay of British Intelligence during the First World War, with other countries, both friend and foe, who did likewise. It was a remarkable step forward and one that showed considerable foresight, by those who recognized the benefits of using women as spies, remembering of course that this was still a time of massive change for women and a journey that had only just begun. Many in the male dominated world could see no further than a woman's place as a wife and mother, or employed in domestic service, yet here these same women were bravely working in stressful and dangerous situations and taking it all in their stride.

Flora Sandes

Flora Sandes has a unique story as far as the First World War is concerned. She was born in Nether Poppleton in Yorkshire on 22 January 1876, although during her childhood, her family moved to Marlesford in Suffolk and from there, on to Thornton Heath in Sussex. She grew up as somewhat of a 'tom boy', enjoying such pastimes as shooting, horse riding and driving.

In 1907 she joined the newly formed First Aid Nursing Yeomanry (FANY), where her riding skills came in handy, as one of the main requirements of joining the organisation was being able to ride a horse. She also had to learn first aid, signaling and drill. In 1910, along with Mabel St Clair Stobart, who she had met through the First Aid Nursing Service, Flora formed the Women's Sick and Wounded Convoy, which in 1912 saw service in Bulgaria and Serbia during the First Balkan War.

The outbreak of the First World War found Flora back in England where she joined the St John Ambulance. Her particular unit had been formed by Mabel Grouitch, who was an American nurse. Flora was one of a group of thirty-six women who left England on 12 August 1914

Flora Sandes in her Serbian army uniform.

en route to Serbia, whose forces were engaged in fighting with troops of the Austro-Hungarian army. Why or how isn't exactly clear, but Flora joined the Serbian Red Cross and ended up being attached to the Serbian army's 2nd Infantry Regiment as an ambulance driver.

In November 1915 Serbian forces, which included the 2nd Infantry Regiment, found themselves in full retreat as they struggled to hold off a joint advance into Serbia by both Bulgarian and Austro-German troops. During this retreat Sandes somehow became separated from her unit and ended up enlisting in the Serbian army, as they were pushed all the way back to the Albanian mountains.

Below is an extract taken from a book written by Sandes that was published in 1916, entitled, *An English Woman Sergeant in the Serbian Army*. She donated the proceeds from the book to the Serbian army:

Later on the next day the sun put in an appearance, as did the Bulgarians. The other side of the mountain was very steep, and our position dominated a flat wooded sort of plateau below, where the enemy were. One of our sentries, who was posted behind a rock, reported the first sight of them, and I went up to see where they were, with two of the officers. I could not see them plainly at first, but they could evidently see our three heads very plainly.

The companies were quickly posted in their various positions, and I made my way over to the Fourth which was in the first line; we did not need any trenches as there were heaps of rocks for cover, and we laid behind them firing by volley. I had only a revolver and no rifle of my own at that time, but one of my comrades was quite satisfied to lend me his and curl himself up and smoke.

By now Sandes had already been promoted to the rank of corporal, an extraordinary achievement, since she was not only female, but a foreigner as well. In early 1916 she was badly wounded during the Serbian army's advance on the Macedonian city of Bitola during the Monastir offensive. During hand-to-hand fighting with the enemy, a grenade exploded nearby and left her with shrapnel embedded in her back and down her right side. She only survived due to the bravery of a colleague who crawled out under enemy fire to rescue her. For her bravery she was awarded Serbia's highest military award, the Order of the Karadorde Star and promoted to the rank of sergeant major.

Because of the severity of her wounds she was unable to be involved in any more fighting, but she remained in the Serbian army and spent the rest of the war running one of the country's military hospitals.

Sandes is the only British woman known to have taken part in active combat during the First World War. At the war's end she was commissioned as a captain, making her the first woman to ever have reached such a rank. She was finally demobilised in 1922.

Flora Sandes had an interesting post war life, one which saw her travelling all over the world, lecturing on her wartime exploits. She found love and happiness when she married one of her fellow officers in May 1927, Yuri Yudenitch. He died in Yugoslavia in September 1941. Sandes later returned to England to live out her life. She died on 24 November 1956 when she was 80 years of age.

Olwen Carey-Evans

Olwen Carey-Evans was another notable female of the First World War, but not so much because of what she did, but of who she was. She was born Olwen Elizabeth Lloyd George in Criccieth, Wales, in 1892, the daughter of David Lloyd George, who in 1916 became the Prime Minister of Great Britain.

At the outbreak of the war she joined the VAD section in her home town and was employed in a nursing capacity as an orderly. Between June and October 1915 she worked at Red Cross Station in Boulogne, before spending a month at Hesdigneul-lès-Béthune, a small farming village in the Pas-de-Calais region of France. From there she returned to England and until June 1916 was working at Devonshire House in Piccadilly in London.

Olwen's VAD service card is somewhat confusing and contradictory. The date she began working for the VAD is shown as being 1914 and the date of when she left is shown as 1919. These have then been crossed out in pencil and replaced with October 1915 and June 1916. As she had started working in Boulogne in June 1915, and was there until October the same year, the penciled in date for when she started with the VAD cannot be correct. The rear of the service card also shows the dates of working for the VAD as being between 1914 and 1919. It also included the following: 'Then at Devonshire House until June 1916, since then she married and has not been able to work.'

In fact it was 19 June 1917 when Olwen married Major Sir Thomas John Carey Evans MC, a lieutenant with the Indian Medical Service. The ceremony took place at the Castle Street Welsh Baptist Church in London. Not only had her name now changed but her place in society had as well. She was no longer Miss Olwen Lloyd George, she was now Lady Carey-Evans.

Violet Constance Jessop

Violet Constance Jessop was born 1 October 1887 in Bahia Blanca, Argentina, the oldest of nine children born to William and Katherine Jessop from Ireland. She arrived in England with her mother and siblings in 1903 after the sudden death of her father. Her mother's job was a stewardess on board ocean going liners. Around 1908 Katherine became ill and had to vacate her position which meant that Violet had no option but to leave her education and go out to work. She chose a life at sea, just as her mother had, which began with the SS *Orinoco*, which was part of the Royal Mail Line, as a stewardess. The year was 1908 and from pictures of her taken at the time, Violet was an extremely attractive 21-year-old woman.

After two years of working on the *Orinoco*, she acquired a similar position working for the White Star Line on board their flag ship vessel, the RMS *Olympic* which plied its trade between Southampton and New York. Between 1911 and 1913, she was the largest ocean going liner in the

RMS *Olympic*.

world, other than during the short working life of her sister ship, the SS *Titanic* in April 1912.

On the evening of 20 September 1911, the *Olympic* raised anchor and set sail, moving slowly and majestically out of Southampton en route to New York with her 2,435 passengers and 950 crew members, one of whom was Violet. This was only the *Olympic*'s fifth voyage.

As the *Olympic* and the British Royal Naval vessel, HMS *Hawke*, were running alongside each other, a collision occurred when the *Olympic* turned to starboard, and the two ships came together. The *Olympic* was left with two large holes in her stern on the starboard side, one above and the other below the water line. Although both ships were badly damaged, there were no fatalities on either vessel.

Violet began working on the RMS *Titanic* as a stewardess on 10 April 1912, just four days before its collision with an iceberg in the North Atlantic. After the order had been given to abandon ship, Violet, according to her memoirs, was tasked with acting as an example to non-English speaking passengers, who could not understand what they were being told and were unclear what was expected of them. Eventually she was ordered to get into lifeboat No. 16 by one of the ship's officers, who then handed her a baby to look after. The next morning her lifeboat was one of those rescued by RMS *Carpathia*. Whilst in somewhat of a daze after

RMS *Olympic* after the collision (*Popular Mechanics* magazine, December 1911).

having survived such an ordeal, she was approached by a woman, who didn't speak to her, but simply snatched the child and ran off. She had no idea who the woman was, but assumed that it was the child's mother.

With the outbreak of the First World War, Violet served with one of the British Red Cross VAD units as a stewardess on board the Olympic Class, HMHS *Britannic*, which before the war had been a passenger liner of the White Star Line, but had subsequently been requisitioned and turned in to a hospital ship.

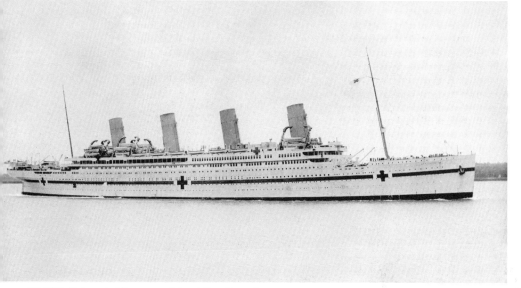

HMHS *Britannic* (Photograph by Allan Green).

On the morning of 21 November 1916 whilst sailing in the Aegean Sea, an unexplained explosion caused it to sink within the space of just fifty-seven minutes. Of those on board thirty were killed, but 1,035 survived, either being rescued from lifeboats or from the sea.

There have been different suggestions put forward as to what caused the *Britannic* to explode. Some say it was a German mine, others that it was a torpedo fired from a German U-boat; the truth has never been established beyond all reasonable doubt. It was the largest vessel to be sunk during the First World War and it is still currently the largest passenger liner, sitting on the sea bed.

Violet's luck held yet again when the lifeboat she was in came very close to being sucked under the *Britannic*'s stern by her propellers; she survived only by jumping out of the lifeboat, sustaining a bad head injury as she did so.

After the end of the First World War when she had finished her VAD commitments, she returned to working for the White Star Line in 1920. She continued her life on the ocean, travelling all over the world whilst working on passenger liners for the White Star Line, the Red Star Line and the Royal Mail Line, finally retiring in 1950.

'Miss Unsinkable', as she was affectionately known by some, died in Great Ashfield, Suffolk in 1971 of congestive heart failure at the age of 83.

Remarkably she was not the only person to survive the same three incidents. Mr Arthur John Priest, a stoker, also holds the same distinction.

CHAPTER SEVEN

THOSE WHO LOST THEIR LIVES

According to the Commonwealth War Graves Commission, a total of 241 women, from six separate nursing organisations, lost their lives whilst serving during the course of the First World War. This chapter is dedicated to these brave women.

Scottish Women's Hospital

The Scottish Women's Hospital was founded in 1914 with the help of financial support provided by both the American Red Cross and the National Union of Women's Suffrage Societies. Soon after the war began their founder, Doctor Elsie Maud Inglis, took the almost unprecedented step for a woman, of contacting the War Office and offering to work with the Royal Army Medical Corps on the Western Front. The offer was turned down in a rather condescending manner, although it must have been blatantly obvious that medical staff were going to be in great demand the longer the war carried on.

Elsie Inglis.

Undeterred, and refusing to take no for an answer, Dr Inglis, took her team of doctors and nurses, ambulance drivers, cooks and orderlies to France, where they set up a 200-bed auxiliary hospital in the thirteenth-century Abaye (Abbey) de Royaumont, working for the French Red Cross. At different times throughout the war, besides France, the Scottish Women's Hospital, had medical facilities in seven other locations including, Serbia, Salonika, Russia, Romania, Corsica, France and Malta.

Serbia in particular remembers the efforts and the bravery of the women who worked for the Scottish Women's Hospital, and each year there is a memorial service held in the city of Kragujevac, which was the Serbian capital, to honour their memory.

During the war Dr Inglis was awarded the Order of Saint Sava, 3rd Class, and the Order of the White Eagle 5th Class, the latter by Crown Prince Alexander of Serbia, at a ceremony in London in April 1916.

With the war finally over the need for organisations such as the Scottish Widows Hospital, was no longer such a necessity. By 1922 they were no more, having wound up their affairs, their members once again returned to the normality of civilian life.

Approximately 1,400 men and women worked for the Scottish Women's Hospital, of whom eleven lost their lives during the war:

Matilda MacDowell is recorded on the Commonwealth War Graves Commission website (CWGC.org) as being a chauffeuse who died on 3 July 1918, whilst serving in Greece. On the Scarlet Finders website (scarletfinders.co.uk) her details are recorded as being Miss Matilda McDowell, chauffeur. She is buried in the Mikra British Cemetery in Kalamaria, which is in the south of the country. The latter part of 1918 saw a worldwide pandemic of influenza, which included an outbreak in the hospitals that were located in Kalamaria. She had worked for the organisation only since 7 May 1918.

Agnes Kerr Earl was 33 years of age and a nursing sister in the American unit, when she died on 19 March 1919. She had been awarded both the Cross of Mercy and the Silver Medal for Devoted Service in War, by the Serbians. She is buried in the Chela Kula Military Cemetery, in Nis, Serbia.

Louisa Jessie Jordan had been with the organisation since 1 December 1914. She was 36 years old and a nursing sister when she died on 6 March 1915. She was also buried in the Chela Kula Military Cemetery in Nis, Serbia. Her parents were from the Maryhill area of Glasgow and her mother, Helen, was a district nurse at Buckhaven, Fife.

Augusta Minshull had only been a nursing sister with the organisation for seven weeks before she died on 1 February 1915. She was another who was buried in the Chela Kula Military Cemetery in Nis, Serbia.

Bessie Gray Sutherland was a nursing sister and 43 years old when she died on 26 September 1915. She is also buried in the Chela Kula Military Cemetery in Nis, Serbia.

Mrs Caroline M. Toughill was a nurse at Mladanovatz and had only been with the organisation since 1 July 1915. She died four months later on 14 November. She is buried in the Skopje British Cemetery which is situated in the Republic of Macedonia. The cemetery was not begun until after the fighting had finished on 11 November 1918, which means that Mrs Toughill was originally buried elsewhere and that her body was subsequently moved to Skopje after the war.

Mary de Burgh Burt was a sister on the Girton and Newnham Unit, based in Salonika. She died on 7 April 1916 and is buried in the Lembet Road Military Cemetery in Salonika. She had joined the organisation on 29 October 1915. At the time of her death, she was attached to the Serbian army.

Florence Missouri Caton enlisted on 4 August 1916 and was a sister on the American section. She died on 15 July 1917. At the time of her death, Florence was attached to the Serbian army. She is also buried in the Lembet Road Military Cemetery in Salonika. Her parents, Captain John Henry and Elizabeth Caton, were from Wrexham in Denbighshire.

Olive Smith was a masseuse on the American unit, and attached to the Serbian army at the time of her death on 24 September 1916. She had originally joined the organisation on 4 August 1916. She is buried in the Lembet Road Military Cemetery in Salonika.

Alice Annie Guy was a sister on the Girton Newnham unit, having joined the organisation on 24 July 1916. At the time of her death, a month later, on 21 August 1916, she was attached to the Serbian army. She was a former superintendent at the Devonshire Hospital in Buxton, Derbyshire. She was buried in the Lembet Road Military Cemetery in Salonika.

All of them were extremely brave women who had a great desire to do what they could for the war effort; how sad then that the War Office decided to turn down the help which the organisation was offering, possibly because of outdated bigotry. Fortunately the French and Serbians realised their worth and were more than grateful for the help they were able to provide.

First Aid Nursing Yeomanry

The First Aid Nursing Yeomanry (FANY), or the Princess Royal's Volunteer Corps, was founded in 1907 and assisted in both nursing and intelligence gathering during the First World War.

Although military in appearance due to the khaki uniform they wore, they were not part of either the regular or reserve army; they were in effect voluntary charity workers.

FANYs serving in France.

The word yeomanry in the title of the unit, is derived from the fact that its members originally worked on horseback, because their founder, Sergeant Major Edward Baker, who was a veteran of both the Sudan campaign, 1881–1899, and the Second Boer War 1899–1902, felt that by being on horseback, the nurses could provide a better service by getting to each wounded man much quicker than if they were on foot. Besides being trained medics, the women were also competent in the art of signalling.

Like their nursing compatriots who were members of the Scottish Women's Hospital, FANYs, received short thrift from the War Office, but they too were not to be deterred in their quest to care for wounded soldiers. They arrived at the French port of Calais in their motorised ambulances on 27 October 1914 and set up hospitals as well as casualty clearing stations, not for the British army, but for the French and Belgians. By the end of the war members of the FANY had been awarded a total of forty-five medals for gallantry whilst carrying out their duties, by the British, French and Belgium authorities. Even though they were not officially recognised by the War Office, their members were awarded seventeen Military Medals.

Evelyn Fidgeon Shaw was the only member of the FANY to die during the war. For her services to France she was awarded the Croix de Guerre with Palm. The citation for her award read as follows:

A volunteer driver of devotion and courage beyond all praise. She exerted herself selflessly, completely disdaining danger and fatigue, whilst carrying out evacuations, often in difficult circumstances and under enemy attacks. She died as a result of a contagion illness contracted in the course of her duty.

She died on 24 August 1918 in France and is buried in the Sezanne Communal Cemetery, which is in the Marne region of France.

The 1911 Census shows her Christian name was spelt as 'Eveline' and that the family's home address was 'St John's', 26 Priory Road, Edgbaston, Birmingham. She was one of five children born to Walter and Julia. Her father was a merchant and manufacturer of horse feed, and the family was wealthy enough to employ two servants and have a home help for her mother who was already 64 years of age.

The following was taken from an Australian blog site on the topic of the First Aid Nursing Yeomanry, predominantly for those Australian women who had been members of the organisation, but it also included this description of Evelyn Fidgeon Shaw and what she did:

Unit VII started work in Epernay in November 1917. By January 1918, during a bitterly cold winter, they had carried 1,817 cases, even though only those absolutely unable to walk were taken in the ambulances. In the big offensive of March 1918 Unit VII carried 1,566 patients. They evacuated wounded soldiers, including many gas cases, to trains, dealt with civilian casualties, and endured nightly air raids.

During the German advance on the Marne in May, 17,000 cases passed through the area in five days. On one day they worked from 4.00am to 8.30pm, filling two trains with 500 patients. They also took the dead to the overflowing mortuary and made dangerous runs with medical supplies and personnel to the front lines. The roads were muddy and shell-pitted, full of refugees, convoys heading to the front, and soldiers in retreat. No lights were allowed on the cars at night, and much of the work was done under fire.

In June 1918 Unit VII moved to Sézanne. During August thousands of gas cases arrived daily; 1,400 alone on the 15th, when the FANY nursed them through the night, even though they had been driving ambulances since 4.00am. Their accommodation was very poor and sanitation was almost non-existent. Many of the women became ill with dysentery, including Evelyn Shaw. She kept working, but soon collapsed and was returned to the mess hut and then the hospital. She suffered a perforated bowel and died on 24 August. She was buried two days later with full military honours.

What a remarkably detailed description of just how hard volunteers like Evelyn worked, not only in the number of hours they put in, but in the extreme circumstances of their work. The fatigue and stress of dealing with wounded soldiers over an extended period of time, some with horrific injuries, must have been extremely traumatic. If that wasn't difficult enough they then had to watch young men die and moments later carry their bodies to a nearby makeshift morgue; it must have been heart-breaking. On many occasions this difficult and emotionally sapping work, would be further compounded by having to endure prolonged and sustained German artillery bombardments.

The British authorities were extremely slow to come to grips with the idea of having women involved in the war so close to the front line, regardless of the proven benefits of the work which they carried out. Because of their indifferent and outdated attitude towards women and nursing, it was not until January 1916, some sixteen months into the war that they finally recognised the value of what the women of the First Aid Nursing Yeomanry provided.

Along with similar voluntary women's organisations, the effective and determined contribution which they provided helped to convince the War Office of the benefits of having women in the services during wartime, and was a factor in the subsequent foundation of the Women's Royal Naval Service and the Women's Army Auxiliary Corps founded in 1917, and the Women's Royal Air Force in 1918.

British Red Cross Society

The primary role of the British Red Cross Society (BRCS) during the First World War was to treat sick and wounded military personnel. Via the Joint War Committee, the BRCS sat side by side with the Order of St John to organise volunteers, as well as professional medical staff, to work in the theatres of war where ever they were.

It was from the Joint War Committee that the Voluntary Aid Detachments (VADs) were born, which carried out such dedicated and sterling work throughout the war years. Besides providing staff, they were also responsible for acquiring properties that could be used as either auxiliary hospitals or convalescent homes for wounded and recovering military

An austere looking group of Red Cross nurses.

personnel. Such premises were set up in local town halls, community halls, large schools and private houses offered by wealthy local residents. Many of these properties had been sourced before the war, which meant that by the time the first wounded soldiers had arrived from Belgium, the auxiliary hospitals and convalescent homes were already up and running, with all of the staff and required equipment in place.

Most of the patients sent to the Red Cross run hospitals and homes, did not have life threatening injuries, but simply needed time to recover and recuperate. The Red Cross was paid by the War Office for every patient that they cared for and the rate was increased for each year of the war. At its peak it was £1.4s.6d for each patient. This covered the cost of their treatment and food.

Most of the staff were men, of whom fifty-four died during the war and one woman, **Winifred Stanley Coates**. Researching her wartime career threw up something of a conundrum; firstly because of the name and the uncertainty as to whether Winifred was in fact a man or a woman; secondly because the CWGC website recorded that Winifred was a nurse with the British Red Cross, whilst Ancestry.co.uk, records her as being a member of the Voluntary Aid Detachment as well as Queen Alexandra's

Red Cross Nurses and patients.

Imperial Military Nursing Service. Even allowing for the direct connection between the Red Cross and the VADs, these subtle variations can make researching and correctly identifying individuals more difficult.

Winifred, was born on 13 February 1889 and at the time of her death on 8 February 1916 was 26 years old. She is buried in the St Helens and Holy Cross Churchyard in Sheriff Hutton, Yorkshire.

She joined the British Red Cross as a nurse on 7 June 1915, serving with the Yorkshire 62nd Detachment. Initially she served at the Royal Infirmary in Bradford, during which time she volunteered for overseas service and was subsequently posted to Malta. On arrival there she served in a Maltese hospital from 2 September 1915, but within only a matter of months, she contracted jaundice and toxaemia, resulting in her having to be sent home where she died on 8 February 1916 in a London Hospital.

She was awarded the British War Medal and the Badge of the Red Cross, 2nd Class.

Queen Alexandra's Imperial Military Nursing Service

Queen Alexandra's Imperial Military Nursing Service (QAIMNS), lost 142 of its members during the First World War.

Staff Nurse (H/1050) Gladys Corfield, was a member of the QAIMNS 2nd Reserve when she died on 6 November 1918, just five days before the

Armistice was signed. She is buried in the Nantmawr Congregational Churchyard, in Shropshire.

Sister Christina Murdoch Wilson, a native of Glasgow, was aged 42 when she died of pneumonia on 1 March 1916. She is buried in the Wimereux Communal Cemetery, which is situated in the Pas de Calais region of France.

Sister Myrtle Elizabeth Wilson was an Australian from Melbourne in Victoria, who at the age of 38, left her homeland to join the QAIMNS in April 1915. Just eight months later on 23 December 1915 she died of pneumonia. She is also buried in the Wimereux Communal Cemetery in France.

Sister Ethel B. Radcliffe was from the picturesque Channel Island of Jersey, but wanting to help the war effort she left her home and enlisted in the QAIMNS. She died on 10 March 1919 and is buried in the Les Baraques Military Cemetery in Sangate, in the Pas de Calais region of France. Her sister, Mrs W. Haig, lived at 'Fair Oaks', Samares, Jersey.

Staff Nurse Ethel Fearnley died on 23 November 1914 with the war still less than four months old. This gave her the regretful distinction of being the first British and Allied nurse to die during the war. At the time of her death she was working at the No. 11 General Hospital at the Imperial Hotel in Boulogne. Time spent there was eloquently described in the book, *A Doctor on the Western Front; The Diary of Henry Owens 1914–1918.*

> I found life here was a complete change in every way. I was able to refresh my memory in medicine and surgery. We bathed in the sea whenever we wanted to.

She is buried in the Boulogne Eastern Cemetery in France. Boulogne was one of the main ports used by the British throughout the First World War and as such had a large number of medical units stationed throughout the area.

Staff Nurse Alice Mary Turton was 36 years old and part of the QAIMNS Special Reserve. At the time of her death on 7 May 1915, she was attached to the 26th Stationary Hospital staff at Ismalia in Egypt. She is buried in the Ismalia War Memorial Cemetery.

Staff Nurse M.H. Johnston was part of 'R' section when she died on 5 September 1915. She is buried in the Cairo War Memorial Cemetery in Egypt.

Probationary Nurse (83/P/481) Edith Dorothy Pepper was 25 when she died on 7 April 1918. She is buried in the Cairo War Memorial Cemetery in Egypt.

Staff Nurse A.C. Reid, aged 32, from Stirlingshire in Scotland, died on 4 March 1919. She is buried in the Cairo War Memorial Cemetery in Egypt.

Staff Nurse Frances E. Brace died on 21 September 1916 and is buried in the Petra Military Cemetery in Malta.

Staff Nurse (C/1037) Mary Clough was part of the unit's 2nd Reserve and 28 years of age when she died on 12 October 1916. She is buried in the Pietra Military Cemetery in Malta. Her family hailed from Blackpool.

Staff Nurse M.A. Walshe died on 21 August 1915 and is buried in the Addolorata Cemetery in Malta.

Sister (H/1339) Sophie Hilling was part of the 2nd Reserve and aged 34 when she died of pneumonia on 12 October 1918. She is buried in Tourgeville Military Cemetery in the Calvados region of France.

Sister S.E. Butler died on 14 April 1916 and is buried in the Alexandria (Chatby) Military and War Memorial Cemetery in Egypt.

Sister Agnes Beryl Corfield was stationed at No. 15 General Hospital in Cairo when she died on 2 February 1916. Like Sister Butler, she is also buried in the Alexandria (Chatby) Military and War Memorial Cemetery in Egypt.

Sister J.L. Griffiths died on 30 October 1915. She is buried in the Alexandria (Chatby) Military and War Memorial Cemetery in Egypt. She was Mentioned in Despatches for her service.

Staff Nurse Lottie M. Stevens died on 15 March 1916 and is buried in Alexandria (Chatby) Military and War Memorial Cemetery in Egypt.

Matron Mary Mitchell MacGill, from Stirling in Scotland, was 32 when she died on 11 March 1915. She is buried in the Aldershot Military Cemetery in Hampshire.

Nurse (O/83) M. O'Brien was a member of the 2nd Reserve when she died on 21 February 1917. She is also buried in the Aldershot Military Cemetery in Hampshire.

Probationer Nurse (83/7564) Constance Emily Mary Seymour was 29 years old when she died of cerebro-spinal meningitis on 12 February

1917. She is buried in the Aldershot Military Cemetery in Hampshire. Her parents were Lord and Lady Ernest Seymour, of The Firs, Kenilworth in Warwickshire.

Staff Nurse (51) Elizabeth Grace Stewart was in the 2nd Reserve when she died on 15 February 1916. She is buried in the Aldershot Military Cemetery in Hampshire. Her family were from Limerick in Ireland.

Staff Nurse Bridget Donovan died on 3 April 1916 and is buried in Portsdown (Christ Church) Military Cemetery in Hampshire.

Staff Nurse Annie Elinor Buckler, aged 43, died of influenza on 17 October 1918. She is buried in the Southampton (Holybrook) Cemetery. She had previously served with the QAIMNS at hospitals in both Malta and Sidcup. Her father was the Rector at Bidston in Cheshire.

Staff Nurse (C/1266) E.K. Cook of the 2nd Reserve, died on 8 September 1917 and is buried in the Alexandria (Hadra) War Memorial Cemetery in Egypt.

Sister (G/689) Alice Jane Grover of the 2nd Reserve, was working at No. 21 General Hospital and was 43 years of age when she died of pneumonia on 6 February 1919. She is buried in the Alexandria (Hydra) War Memorial Cemetery.

Probationer Nurse (83/11/107) Nellie Hawley was attached to HMS *Osmanieh*, which was commanded by Lieutenant Commander David R. Mason of the Royal Naval Reserve, when it was sunk on 31 December 1917 at the entrance to Alexandria Harbour by a mine laid by the German submarine, UC-34, under the command of Oberleutnant zur See, Horst Obermueller. The mine struck the starboard side of the ship, amidships, causing her to sink. On board that fateful day were troops and a number of medical staff who were on their way to Egypt. A total of 209 people, including Nellie and seven other nurses, were amongst the dead. The other nurses were: **Catherine Ball**, **Winifred Maud Brown**, **Gertrude Bytheway**, **Lilian Midwood**, **Staff Nurse (R/853) Margaret Dorothy Roberts**, **Hermione Angela Rogers** and **Una Duncanson**.

Having been launched in 1906 as a passenger ship, HMS *Osmanieh* was requisitioned by the Admiralty at the outbreak of the war and became a 'Fleet Messenger' supplying stores and personnel from one location to another.

Some six months earlier on 23 June 1917, HMS *Osmanieh* had been attacked by a German submarine which fired two torpedoes at her, but thankfully for those on board the vessel, both missed.

HMS *Osmanieh*.

Matron (2/P/193) Elizabeth Kelly Parker was from Castlemoor, County Kilkenny in Ireland. She died of dysentery on 16 October 1916 and is buried in the Alexandria (Hadra) War Memorial Cemetery.

Sister Elsie Mabel Gladstone was 32 when she died of pneumonia on 24 January 1919. She is buried in the Belgrade Cemetery in the Namur region of France.

Nursing Sister Marjorie Croysdale was 26 years old when she died on 2 March 1919. She is buried in the Etaples Military Cemetery in the Pas de Calais region of France.

Matron Eveline Maud Dawson, aged 49, died on 10 April 1917 and is buried in the Etaples Military Cemetery.

Nursing Sister Jeanie Barclay Smith was 42 years old when she died on 28 April 1916. She had been awarded the Royal Red Cross Medal 1st Class. She is also buried in the Etaples Military Cemetery.

Sister Emily Helena Cole, aged 32, died on 2 September 1915. She is buried in the Wimereux Communal Cemetery, in the Pas de Calais region of France.

Sister Isabella Lucy May Duncan was attached to the 13th Stationary Hospital at Boulogne. She died on 1 March 1917 and is also buried in the Wimereux Communal Cemetery in France.

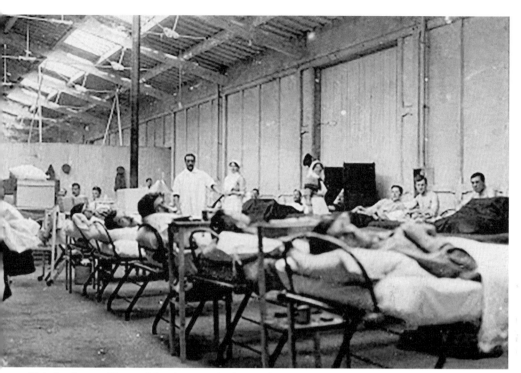

13th Stationary Hospital Boulogne. The hospital was set up in large industrial sheds by the harbour, in Boulogne, which logistically made it both easy and convenient to move wounded men from their hospital bed to a nearby hospital ship waiting in the harbour to take them back home to England.

Sister Jessie Olive Hockey, aged 32, was a South African by birth. Her parents lived in the country's Cape Province. Jessie died on 14 August 1917 and is also buried in the Wimereux Communal Cemetery.

Florence D'Oyly Compton was 29 years old and working at the 65th British General Hospital in Basra, Iraq, when she died by drowning on 15 January 1918. She is buried in the Basra War Cemetery.

Nursing Sister I.M. Kearney died on 26 September 1916 and is buried in the Basra War Cemetery in Iraq.

Staff Nurse C.M.F. Kemp was working at the 40th British General Hospital in Basra when she died on 4 July 1918. She was buried in the Basra War Cemetery.

Staff Nurse (670) Susie Marie Colbourn Smith, aged 37, was a member of the 2nd Reserve when she died on 12 February 1916. She is buried in Wolverhampton Borough Cemetery.

Staff Nurse (H/784) F. Hawley was part of the 2nd Reserve when she died on 20 June 1918. She is buried in the Burslem Cemetery in Stoke-on-Trent.

Probationer Nurse F.M. Bates died on 9 April 1916 and is buried in the Reigate Cemetery in Surrey.

Dorothy Maud Chandler was 31 years of age and working at the Queen Alexandra's Military Hospital at Millbank, London, which was first opened in July 1905, when she died on 15 November 1917. She had previously served with the 26th General Hospital at Etaples in France. She is buried in Epsom Cemetery in Surrey. The family home was in Cheam, Surrey.

Staff Nurse (C/747) Elizabeth Annie Challinor, aged 29, was a member of the 2nd Reserve when she died of pneumonia on 26 October 1918. She is buried in the Stoke Old Cemetery in Guildford. Her parents Samuel and Sarah Challinor, lived at 'Thelma', Caxton Garden, Guildford.

Staff Nurse (B562) Laurie Edna Bird was just 29 years of age and a member of the 2nd Reserve when she died suddenly of heart failure on 19 August 1919. She is buried in Brookwood Cemetery in Surrey which has 138 Commonwealth war graves from the First World War, most of these being patients and staff from the Millbank Military Hospital in London.

Sister (E/20) Margaret Elliffe, aged 27, was part of the 2nd Reserve. She died on 24 May 1916 and is also buried in Brookwood Cemetery.

Staff Nurse (H/280) Ida Durrant Hannaford was 34 when she died on 14 March 1918. Originally from Birmingham, her widowed mother was living in Canada by the end of the war. Ida is also buried in Brookwood Cemetery.

Staff Nurse (L/5) Hilda Louisa Lea aged 38 was serving with the 2nd Reserve when she died on 10 May 1916. She too is buried in the Brookwood Cemetery.

Sister C. Nicol, from Caithness in Scotland, was part of the 2nd Reserve, and 34 years old when she died on 6 February 1916. She is buried in Brookwood Cemetery.

Sister (S/660) Gertrude Annie Stephenson who was part of the 2nd Reserve, was aged 42 when she died on 25 March 1918. She is also buried in Brookwood Cemetery.

Staff Nurse (S/101) Kate Rosina Sturt from London, was 28 years old when she died on 13 December 1916. She is buried in Brookwood Cemetery.

Staff Nurse (T/95) Edith Sarah Tulloch was part of the 2nd Reserve when she died on 8 October 1918. She was 33 years old and was buried in Brookwood Cemetery.

Staff Nurse (W/72) Lillie Wallace, another member of the 2nd Reserve who is buried in Brookwood Cemetery. She died on 6 June 1916.

Staff Nurse (B/1257) Katie Bolger was born in County Carlow in Ireland in 1886. She was a member of the 2nd Reserve and 30 years old when she died on 5 March 1916. She is buried in the grounds of St John's Parish Church in Sutton Venny, Wiltshire. The churchyard has 168 First World War graves, 143 of which are Australian. Sutton Veny had a large military presence during the First World War which explains the number of graves at the church. The 26th Division was based in the area during April 1915 and the No. 1 Australian Command was there from the latter part of 1916 to October 1919. After the signing of the Armistice the No. 1 Australian General Hospital was situated there and there was also a hutted military hospital which could cater for some 1,200 patients.

Sister Elizabeth Robertson Thomson was 36 years old when she died on 26 October 1918. She worked at Leith War Hospital run by Queen Alexandra's Imperial Nursing Service and as buried in Edinburgh's Rosebank Cemetery.

For a few months between August and October 1918 Leith was home to an American Naval Hospital which had been set up in the town's Poor House, which eventually became the Eastern General Hospital. The premises had been requisitioned earlier in the war by the British army for use as one of their own military hospitals, but in August 1918, they handed it over to the United States navy and it then became the United States Navy Base Hospital No. 3.

The staff for the hospital were nearly all American, having been sent over from the California Hospital in Los Angeles, arriving in England by ship at Liverpool after a two week journey, on 15 August 1918. Their voyage across the Atlantic had begun in New York on 1 August 1918 and had then taken them to Halifax in Nova Scotia. For their own safety they then joined a convoy and made their way across the Atlantic, finally arriving in Leith. The hospital initially had enough space and beds for 750 patients. Wooden huts were added to increase the capacity of the hospital so that it could comfortably cater for 1,000 patients.

The hospital's patients were not all Americans, nor were they exclusively naval personnel. About three quarters of them were British soldiers. Most of the American personnel who were patients at the hospital, had been stricken with influenza. The hospital was very busy during its short existence but with the signing of the Armistice on 11 November 1918, it was quickly shut down.

Staff Nurse Nellie Willson was a Lincolnshire girl from Billinghay. She was 30 years of age when she died on 16 October 1918 and is buried in St Michael's Parish Church Cemetery in Billinghay.

Sister (B1302) Ella Maud Bond was from Southport and was serving with the Second Reserve, when she died on 3 November 1918, aged 31. She had been awarded the Associate Royal Red Cross Medal. She is buried in the Scartho Road Cemetery in Grimsby.

Sister (C/349) E.F.M.C. Callier was part of the 2nd Reserve when she died on 22 June 1919. She is buried in Greenwich Cemetery.

Sister (G/544) Martha Gorbutt, a member of the 2nd Reserve, served on board HMHS *Nevasa*. She died 28 July 1920 and is buried in Greenwich Cemetery in London. The *Nevasa* was launched on 12 December 1912 as a passenger liner which plied its trade between London, East Africa and India. She was owned by the British India Steam Navigation Company. At the outbreak of the war she was commandeered and converted into a troop ship, before becoming a hospital ship in January 1915, capable of accommodating 660 beds.

Sister Lena Crowther died on 22 October 1916 and is buried in the Tottenham Cemetery in Middlesex.

Sister (G/198) A.E.C. Garner was in the 2nd Reserve when she died on 12 March 1917. She is also buried in the Tottenham Cemetery.

Sister Ada Marion Johnson, aged 24, died on 24 October 1918 and was buried in Tottenham Cemetery. The family home was at New Malden in Surrey.

Nurse Catherine Meikle, aged 23, died 14 October 1918, only ten days before Sister Johnson. Like her colleague she was buried in the Tottenham Cemetery.

Florence Nightingale Shore, who was related to the Crimean nurse Florence Nightingale, and a holder of the Associate Royal Red Cross Medal, died on 16 January 1920. She is buried in the Hanwell Cemetery in the City of Westminster.

Staff Nurse (T/66) Eugene Elizabeth Teggin was 28 years old and part of the 2nd Reserve, when she died just six weeks after the signing of the

Armistice, on Christmas Day 1918. She is buried in St Martin's Church-yard in Shropshire.

Nursing Sister W.M. Harrison died on 3 April 1920 and is buried in the Trimulgherry Cantonment Cemetery in India.

Sister Helen Milne was 31 years old when she died on 23 November 1917. Her name is commemorated on the Kirkee 1914–1918 Memorial, which is situated near the town Poona, near Bombay. The memorial was built to commemorate the service men and women who died or were killed during the First World War and who were initially buried in other cemeteries throughout India and Pakistan.

Nurse Ada Moreton was 38 years of age when she died on 7 September 1916. She is buried in the Kirkee Memorial in India.

Matron Frances Mary Hall, aged 45, died on 7 July 1919. She had been awarded the Royal Red Cross Medal and was Mentioned in Despatches. Her name is commemorated on the India Gate Delhi Memorial and she is buried in the Peshawar British Cemetery. She had previously served in the South African War as well as in Egypt, Salonika and Mesopotamia.

Staff Nurse Nellie Spindler, aged 26, was killed in action on 21 August 1917. She was stationed at the 44th Casualty Clearing Station in Brad-hoek. Such facilities are usually situated a safe distance away from the front line fighting, offering an element of protection for patients and staff. Unfortunately for Nellie, the CCS was close to a railway line and an ammunition dump, which made it a prime target. On 21 August the base came under artillery bombardment, which resulted in one of the shells landing close to Nellie. She was critically wounded and died from her wounds later that day. She is buried in the Lijssenthoek Military Cemetery in the West-Vlaanderen region of Belgium.

Staff Nurse (T/91) Lilian Thomas, aged 27, was part of the 2nd Reserve when she died on 14 August 1918. She is buried in Toxteth Park Cemetery in Liverpool.

Sister Anne Cooper died on 17 November 1919, aged 38. Her dedication to her work resulted in her being Mentioned in Despatches. She is buried in Manchester Crematorium.

Staff Nurse (S/1235) F.E. Smith was part of the 2nd Reserve when she died on 1 July 1918. She had previously worked at the Military Hospital in Aylesbury. She is buried in Gorton Cemetery in Manchester. Before the war the premises for the hospital were Aylesbury Grammar School, but in

October 1914 it was requisitioned by the War Office and transformed into Aylesbury Military Hospital. By the end of the war, twenty-one former pupils of the school had become victims of the bloody conflict.

Staff Nurse Mary Ann Allen was 35 years of age and from Tyldesley in Manchester. She died on 5 January 1920 and is buried in Tyldesley Cemetery.

Staff Nurse Helena Stewart Bennett died on 18 October 1918 and is buried in the Arbroath Western Cemetery.

Staff Nurse M.S. Dewar, who had previously been Mentioned in Despatches for her quality and standard of work, died on 12 March 1917. She is buried in the Mirka British Cemetery in Kalamaria, Greece.

Staff Nurse Margaret Ellison Duckers was aged 25 when she died on 16 May 1918. Her family home was in Wetheral, Carlisle. She was also buried in the Mirka British Cemetery, in Kalamaria.

Sister Eveline Mary Hodgson was attached to the 28th General Hospital in Macedonia, when she died of malaria, five weeks after the signing of the Armistice, on 21 December 1918. She had previously served on board HMHS *Letitia*. She is buried in the Mirka British Ceremony at Kalamaria in Greece. During the course of the war, Mirka had eighteen general and stationary hospitals located in the town.

Staff Nurse Mary Bethia Marshall was aged 30 years when she died on 12 March 1917 during an air raid by German bombers. She had previously been Mentioned in Despatches and awarded the Croix de Guerre with Palms by France for her brave and excellent work in extremely trying circumstances. She is also buried in the Mirka British Cemetery in Kalamaria.

Staff Nurse Martha Townsend died on 21 September 1918. She is buried in the Mirka British Cemetery in Kalamaria, Greece. Her parents, Mr and Mrs James Townsend, lived at 'Redwalls', Rollstones Road, Writtle, Chelmsford, Essex.

Sister Ellen Armstrong was 38 years old when she died on 20 March 1919. She was Mentioned in Despatches and had also received the Associate Royal Red Cross medal for her work. She is buried in the St Sever Cemetery in Rouen, France.

Staff Nurse Elizabeth Harvey Watson who was from County Down in Ireland, was 30 years of age when she died of pneumonia on 5 November

1918, less than a week before the Armistice was signed. She is buried in the Caudry British Cemetery in the Nord region of France. Within weeks of the outbreak of the war, the town of Caudry was in German hands, where it became one of their major medical centres. That is how it stayed until it was captured by troops of the 37th British Army Division on 10 October 1918. The medical theme stayed after its belated capture with units from the 3rd, 19th, 21st and 49th Casualty Clearing Stations being positioned in and around the town.

Sister Mary Agnes Doherty was from County Derry in Ireland. She was 28 years of age at the time of her death on 5 September 1916 from dysentery, and is buried in the Lembet Road Military Cemetery in Salonika, Greece. She had been awarded the Associate Royal Red Cross Medal for her devotion to her profession.

Staff Nurse Jessie Richie was from Perthshire in Scotland. She died on 13 August 1916. She is also buried in the Lembet Road Military Cemetery in Salonika, Greece.

Sister F. Tindall was attached to the 65th British General Hospital when she died by drowning on 15 January 1918. She is buried in the Basra War Cemetery, in what is today Iraq, but during in the First World War, was Mesopotamia. The circumstances of her death are that she was in a party of a matron and twelve other nursing staff who had been invited to spend an afternoon at the Beit Naana officer's hospital, to meet with the wounded officers and to take afternoon tea. Their journey from Basra was by motor launch. After an enjoyable interlude away from the hustle and bustle of their everyday working existence, they were returning to the 65th British General Hospital in Basra, when tragedy struck in the form of a collision with another vessel. Four of the nurses from the launch, including Sister Tindall, were killed.

Sister Alice Welford aged 30, also drowned in the same incident as Sister Tindall. A subsequent Court of Enquiry decided that the deaths of the nurses were accidental due to an error of judgement by the steersman of the launch.

Chief Matron Beatrice Isabel Jones CBE, was 54 years of age when she died on 14 January 1921. She had been awarded the Associate Royal Red Cross medal along with the Nightingale International Medal. She is buried in the North Gate War Cemetery in Baghdad.

Staff Nurse Hannah Elizabeth Wright died just three weeks before the signing of the Armistice, on 22 October 1918, of pneumonia. She is buried in Staglieno Cemetery in Genoa, Italy. For the last year of the war, British medical units were located in the Italian city in the form of the 11th British General Hospital as well as the 38th and 51st Stationary Hospitals.

Staff Nurse Rachel Ferguson from County Derry in Ireland, died of pneumonia on 26 June 1918, whilst working at the 62nd General Hospital in Bordighera. She is buried in the Bordighera British Cemetery in Italy.

Nursing Sister Charlotte Berrie, was 32 years old when she died on 8 January 1919. She is buried in the Jerusalem War Cemetery.

Staff Nurse A.M. Russell died on 4 October 1916 and is buried in Reading Cemetery.

Staff Nurse Mary Danaher was from County Limerick in Ireland, and aged 26 when she died on 12 October 1918. Her final resting place is at the Gaza War Cemetery.

Sister Annie Glendhill was 43 years of age when she died on 17 October 1918 and is buried in the Gaza War Cemetery.

Sister (B/506) E.L. Brown died on 19 February 1919 and is buried in the Bear Road Cemetery in Brighton.

Sister R.A. McGibbon from County Armagh in Ireland died on 6 March 1919 and is buried in the Dougher Roman Catholic Cemetery in Lurgan.

Sister (T/417) Christina Jack served with the 2nd Reserve and was a holder of the Associate Royal Red Cross medal. She died on 22 October 1918 aged 35 and is buried in the Mount Vernon Cemetery at Thurso in Scotland.

Nurse (M/1473) I. MacKenzie was a member of the 2nd Reserve when she died on 2 November 1918, just nine days before the signing of the Armistice. She is buried in the Melness Cemetery in Tongue, Scotland.

Staff Nurse (W/969) Katherine Williams was 38 years of age and serving with the 2nd Reserve when she died on 4 August 1919. She is buried in the Bronynant Cemetery in Colwyn Bay in Wales.

Staff Nurse E. Roberts died on 12 August 1917 and is buried in Rhyl Town Cemetery.

Matron M. Farley was a holder of the Associate Royal Red Cross medal. She died on 1 June 1918 and is buried in the Mount Jerome Cemetery in Dublin, Ireland.

Sister Edith Mary Oxley was 45 years of age when she died of influenza on 12 December 1918. She is buried in the Pioneer Cemetery in Harare, Zimbabwe.

Sister Florence Narrelle Hobbes was 45 years of age when she died on 10 May 1918. Her name is commemorated on the Basra Memorial. When war broke out Florence was matron of a hospital in New South Wales, Australia. Rather than wait to enlist with the Australian forces she went to England to join QAIMNS and served during the ill-fated Gallipoli Campaign in 1915. Later she went on to work in Sicily, India and Mesopotamia and by 1917 had become ill. Her family sent her youngest sister, Elsie, to bring her home. As they made their way home to Australia on the hospital ship *Kanowna* Florence died, with her sister by her side, and was buried at sea.

Nursing Sister (D/369) A.E. Dawes was serving with the 2nd Reserve when she died on 23 October 1918. She is buried in Foster Hill Road Cemetery in Bedford.

Sister (R/13) Annie Louise Roberts was serving with the 2nd Reserve, when she died on 28 September 1916 and is buried in the Flaybrick Hill Cemetery in Birkenhead, Cheshire.

Staff Nurse Constance Harriet Partridge was 42 years old when she died on 5 January 1920. She is buried in the Ventnor Cemetery on the Isle of White.

Staff Nurse Clara McAlister, aged 36, died on 10 April 1917. She was on board HMHS *Salta* when it struck a mine and sank. Her body was never recovered, but her name is recorded and commemorated on a memorial at the Ste Marie Cemetery at Le Havre in France.

Sister Rebecca McMurray Munro, aged 32 and from Forfarshire in Scotland was a holder of the Associate Royal Red Cross medal. She died on 30 April 1920 and her body was laid to rest at the Rosehill Cemetery in Montrose, Scotland.

Staff Nurse (R40618) Nellie Saw was 29 years old when she died on 31 March 1920. She is buried in the Old Public Cemetery in Albany, Western Australia.

Sister Bessie Harkness was 26 years old and originally from Scotland. She died on 11 April 1919 and is buried in the Crosshill Cemetery in Ayrshire.

Staff Nurse Emily Gray, aged 30, died on 16 January 1919. She is buried in her native Ireland at the Minterburn Presbyterian Church graveyard, in County Tyrone.

Staff Nurse Blanche Atkinson was 38 years old and a holder of the Associate Royal Red Cross medal. She died on 9 December 1919 and is buried in the Stirling District Cemetery in Southern Australia.

Staff Nurse (R/S/519) Dorothy Louise Stacey, 25 years old, died on 5 October 1918 and is buried in the Sherborne Cemetery in Dorset.

Nursing Assistant (H/84) F.M.L. Hook died the day before the signing of the Armistice, on 10 November 1918. She is buried in Weymouth Cemetery in Dorset.

Staff Nurse V.C. Consterdine died just five days before the signing of the Armistice, on 6 November 1918, and is buried in Nottingham Church Cemetery.

Sister (2D/147) J.G. Dalton died on 20 March 1916 and is buried in the Kilbride Parish Churchyard in Argyllshire, Scotland.

Sister (S/136) M.B. Stalker was serving with 1st Reserve when she died on 18 January 1921, and is buried in Comrie Cemetery in Perthshire, Scotland.

Nurse (M/636) Jessie Elizabeth McRobbie was 32 years of age and serving with the 2nd Reserve, when she died just four days before the signing of the Armistice, on 7 November 1918. She is buried in Crief Cemetery in Perthshire, Scotland.

Nurse (W1022) M. Watson was serving with the 2nd Reserve at the time of her death on 6 November 1918, and is also buried in Crief Cemetery.

Staff Nurse (M1009) Margaret Ann Macbeth was 28 years old and part of the 2nd Reserve when she died on 30 October 1918. She is buried in Pitlochry Cemetery in Perthshire, Scotland.

Acting Matron Katy Beaufoy, who was a veteran of the Second Boer War (1899–1902), died on 26 February 1918. She was on board HMHS *Glenart Castle* when it was struck at 4.00am, by a torpedo fired by the German Submarine *UC-56*, and sank soon after, having left Newport in South Wales en route to Brest in France. A total of 162 people were killed including Captain Bernard Burt, eight nurses, seven medical officers from the Royal Army Medical Corps and forty-seven medical orderlies.

HMHS *Glenart Castle*.

The following information about the sinking of the *Glenart Castle* is taken from Wikipedia:

> Evidence was found suggesting that the submarine may have shot at initial survivors of the sinking in an effort to cover up the sinking of *Glenart Castle*. The body of a junior officer of *Glenart Castle* was recovered from the water close to the position of the sinking. It was marked with two gunshot wounds, one in the neck and the other in the thigh. The body also had a life vest indicating he was shot while in the water.
>
> After the war the British Admiralty sought the captains of U-boats who sank hospital ships, in order to charge men with war crimes. Kapitanleutnant Wilhelm Keisewetter, the Commander of *UC-56*, when the *Glenart Castle* was sunk, was arrested after the war on his voyage back to Germany and interned in the Tower of London. He was released on the grounds that Britain had no right to hold a detainee during the Armistice.

Kiesewetter and the crew of *UC-56*, had all been interned in neutral Spain after arriving in Santander on 24 May 1918 badly damaged, which was before his arrest by the British authorities. He was an experienced officer, having first enlisted in the German military on 25 November 1901. The *Glenart Castle* was the only Allied vessel that Kiesewetter and *UC-56* sank during his time in charge of her, between 1 February 1917 and 24 May 1918.

It does not appear that he was ever charged with war crimes for his actions on 26 February 1918, in sinking the clearly lit hospital ship as he was still serving in the German Navy until 21 January 1920.

He served his country again during the Second World War, becoming the oldest submarine commander in the world, at 62 years of age.

Katy Beaufoy's body was never recovered and she is presumed to have drowned. Her name is commemorated on the Hollybrook Memorial at Southampton.

The following nurses also died on the *Glenart Castle* and are commemorated on the Hollybrook Memorial: **Staff Nurse Rebecca Rose Beresford**, aged 39; **Staff Nurse Edith Blake**, 32 years old and from Sans Souci in Sydney Australia; **Staff Nurse Elizabeth Edgar** was a senior sister staff nurse and had lived at 1 Grove Place, Redland, Bristol; **Sister Jane Evans** was the daughter of Evan and Mary Rebecca Evans; **Staff Nurse Charlotte E. Henry** was 41 and had been trained at South Devon and Cornwall Hospital in 1905 after which she held various nursing posts before joining QAIMNS; **Sister Rose Elizabeth Kendall** was also killed in the sinking of the *Glenart Castle* and is also commemorated on the Hollybrook Memorial at Southampton.

Sister J. Phillips died on 21 March 1917 when she drowned at sea whilst serving on board HMHS *Asturias*. On 20 March 1917 the *Asturias* was en route from Avonmouth in Bristol to Southampton, when she was struck by a torpedo fired by the German submarine *UC-66*.

The *Asturias* was launched in 1908 and was owned by the Royal Mail Steam Packet Company, running between Southampton and Buenos Aires in Argentina. After the outbreak of the war she was requisitioned by the War Office for use as a hospital ship. The *Asturias* had previously been struck by a torpedo fired by a German U-boat, on 1 February 1915, which failed to explode. On 20 March 1917, good fortune was once again with the *Asturias*, as the 1,000 wounded men who had been on board had been disembarked at Avonmouth. Thankfully, she did not sink and the captain managed to beach her near Bolt Head, a headland on the south coast of Devon. A total of thirty-one of those on board were killed, with a further twelve recorded missing. Amongst the dead were nursing staff, crew and members of the Royal Army Medical Corps.

HMHS *Asturias*.

Staff Nurse Mary Rodwell died on 17 November 1915 and her name is commemorated on the Hollybrook Memorial at Southampton. Nurse Rodwell was one of those who were on board HMHS *Anglia* when she struck a mine just east of Folkestone. The mine in question had been laid by the German submarine *UC-5*. The *Anglia* was carrying 390 wounded officers and men from Calais to Dover, when it hit the mine and sank quickly beneath the waves, taking 134 of those on board to a watery grave.

Sister (J/110) Lilian Hilda Jones was 32 years of age when she died of pneumonia on 28 October 1918. Although born in London, she is buried in the Ford Park Cemetery in Plymouth, Devon.

Staff Nurse Helen Hetterley, aged 26, died on 30 May 1917 and is buried in the Oakham Cemetery in Rutland.

Probationary Nurse Doris Ellen Pilling was 24 years old when she died of pneumonia on 28 March 1919. A London girl, she was buried in the Hammersmith Old Cemetery.

Matron Maude Amy Buckingham was 42 years old when she died on 4 December 1915. She is buried in the All Souls Cemetery, Kensal Green in London. During her service with the QAIMNS, she was in charge of the Queen's Hospital in Birmingham as well as the 2nd War Hospital at Holymoor, Birmingham.

Nurse (M/813) M. Marmion, aged 37, was a member of the 2nd Reserve, when she died on 25 January 1919. She is buried in the St Mary's Roman Catholic Cemetery in Kensal Green.

Nursing Sister Isabella Cruickshank, aged 48, died 10 April 1917. She hailed from Aberdeen in Scotland. Her name is commemorated on the Salta Memorial in Ste Marie Cemetery in Le Havre, France, in memory of those who lost their lives when HMHS *Salta* was sunk by a mine near the port. The death toll included nine nurses, seventy-nine crew as well as forty-two members of the Royal Army Medical Corps. All the following nurses are casualties of the *Salta* and remembered on the same memorial.

Nursing Sister Ellen Lucy Foyster, aged 36.

Staff Nurse Elizabeth Shepherd Gurney is also remembered on the Merseyside Roll of Honour.

Nursing Sister Gertrude Eileen Jones aged 31.

Staff Nurse Fanny Mason, aged 27.

Staff Nurse Jane Roberts was a head teacher's daughter from Dolgellau, Meirionnydd in Wales.

Staff Nurse Agnes Greig Mann, aged 25, was the daughter of Mr and Mrs John Mann, of 17, Clepington St., Dundee.

Staff Nurse Phyllis Ada Pearse was 28 years old when she died of neurasthenia, the symptoms of which include, fatigue, anxiety, headaches, heart palpitations, high blood pressure and a depressed mood, on 29 April 1915. She is buried in the Ste Marie Cemetery in Le Havre, France.

Staff Nurse (R/741) Caroline Amelia Robinette, 2nd Reserve, died on 30 March 1917. She was a holder of the Associate Royal Red Cross medal and is buried in Herne Bay Cemetery, in Kent.

Sister Stella Rose Boue-Blandy, aged 32, died on 13 January 1919, and is buried in the Birkdale Cemetery in Lancashire. Her brother, Claude Reginald Boue-Blandy, had initially enlisted in the Manchester Regiment, before taking a commission as a second lieutenant with the 5th Battalion, South Lancashire Regiment. According to Bruce Hubbard's book, *Ainsdale War Memorial* Claude's health deteriorated whilst serving in France and he was returned to the UK, where he was admitted to a hospital in Bangor, which is believed to be the Penrhyn Cottage VAD hospital. He died of a pneumonia related heart attack, on 18 April 1916. Like his sister Stella, he is buried in the Birkdale Cemetery.

As can be seen by the deaths of the brave young women mentioned above, just as many of them died from illness and disease, as they did from been lost at sea or from artillery bombardments.

Queen Alexandra's Royal Naval Nursing Service

Queen Alexandra's Royal Naval Nursing Service lost ten of their nurses during the First World War.

Sister Mabel Edith Grigson was 36 years of age and stationed at the Royal Naval Hospital in Malta when she died on 3 October 1918. She is buried in the Capuccini Naval Cemetery in Malta.

Nursing Sister Eva Gladys Beard was 33 years of age when she died on 14 March 1920. She is buried in the Churchyard of Christ Church, Upper Tean in Staffordshire.

Nursing Sister Mary Jennette Robins, aged 28, was stationed at Chatham when she died of pneumonia on 4 November 1918. She is buried in the churchyard of St Mary's in Mellor, Lancashire.

Sister A. Wilson died on 5 November 1918 and is buried in the Monymusk Parish Churchyard, in Aberdeenshire, Scotland.

Nursing Sister G.A. Ainsworth was stationed at the Royal Naval Hospital in Peebles when she died on 29 October 1918. She is buried in Peebles cemetery.

Nursing Sister Annette Maud Prevost was stationed at the Royal Naval Hospital at Chatham, when she died on 19 November 1918. She is buried in the Woodlands Cemetery in Gillingham, Kent.

Nursing Sister Louisa Charlotte Chamberlain was serving on board HMHS *China* when it struck a mine in Scapa Flow on 10 August 1918. The resulting explosion killed three of those on board, one being Sister Chamberlain. Because of the location of the incident, there is debate as to whether it was a German mine set up to catch British ships on their way out of the harbour, or a British one, intended to stop German submarines from getting in.

On the afternoon of 30 December 1915 the Hospital Ship, HM *Natal*, a Warrior Class cruiser, was at anchor in the Cromarty Firth. Her commander, Captain Eric Black, was hosting a party aboard and had invited the wives and children of all of his officers, a friend of his and their family and nurses from the Hospital Ship HM *Drina* which was anchored nearby. During the party there was a massive internal explosion.

A total of 421 of the crew and their family members were killed, and some 400 of the crew survived. Amongst the dead were three members of Queen Alexandra's Royal Naval Nursing Service. They were: **Nursing**

HMS *Natal*.

Sister Caroline Maud Edwards; **Nursing Sister Eliza Millicent Elvens**; and **Nursing Sister Olive Kathleen Rowlett**. None of their bodies were recovered, but their names are recorded on the Chatham Naval Memorial.

Voluntary Aid Detachments

Voluntary Aid Detachments were born out of an amalgamation of efforts between the British Red Cross and the Order of St John, in August 1909.

With Britain having been involved in the Second Boer War of 1899–1902, and with the growing threat of a European war in the following years, the concern was that there would be a shortage of nurses to deal with the wounded. The idea was that the Voluntary Aid Detachments, would provide basic nursing and administrative assistance to military and other full time professional nurses, thus allowing them to concentrate fully on the medical aspect of their role.

In just two years some 20,000 volunteers had been encouraged to enrol in a total of 659 detachments located up and down the country. By the start of the First World War the number of volunteers had risen to over 70,000, with some 2,500 detachments, but despite this enthusiasm, there were some issues that needed to be addressed before these volunteers could be effectively deployed. Many of the women were from the middle and upper classes of society, and hadn't even encountered bad language in their lives, let alone the tough hospital discipline that they would now have to accept.

At the outbreak of war, and in readiness for the expected large number of wounded soldiers who would be returned to Britain to be treated, VADs were deployed to work on the wards of many of the military hospitals located around the country. They were also largely responsible for the setting up and running of the numerous convalescent hospitals which were needed to allow the wounded men to recuperate, before most of them were returned to military service.

The other issue was the refusal of military authorities to allow VADs anywhere near the front line. In some cases this was because of concerns about their actual abilities and in others it was born out of a belief that women in general should not be exposed to such pain and suffering, as they simply would not be able to emotionally deal with the trauma of what they saw.

Even the British Red Cross had its concerns about allowing female civilians to work in overseas military hospitals.

By the end of 1914 VAD nurses had been deployed overseas, but only to work in such roles as cooks or waitresses. Some historians describe there being a shortage of trained nurses, in those early months of the war, whilst others take the view that it was down to the unexpectedly high number of casualties that simply overwhelmed the number of nurses that were available. Either way, this inadvertently opened the door for VAD nurses to be used in an overseas capacity, with military personnel who had previously been against their deployment in military hospitals, now only too grateful for their assistance. The British Red Cross imposed their own restrictions on who could serve overseas, making such postings only available to women who were 23 years of age and who had at least three months experience of working in a hospital. By the end of the war an estimated 38,000 VAD nurses had worked throughout the Western Front, the Eastern Front, Gallipoli and Mesopotamia. They had certainly proved their worth, with hundreds of them receiving awards for gallantry as well as being Mentioned in Despatches.

According to the Commonwealth War Graves Commission, seventy-eight VAD members died or were killed as a result of their First World War service.

Volunteer Mrs Ruby Pickard was 67 years of age when she died of stomach cancer on 13 April 1916. She was the wife of Captain Pickard, and the couple lived at St Leonard, Pont de Briques, Pas de Calais, France. She was a British Red Cross voluntary worker whose role it was to supply British hospitals with daily newspapers. She is buried in the Wimereux Communal Cemetery, near Boulogne. Her touching epitaph reads, 'Rests here with those she tried to comfort'.

Chauffeuse Helen Maud Peel was 22 years of age and worked for her local Sunningdale VAD. She died on 13 December 1917 and is buried in the Holy Trinity Churchyard at Sunningdale, Berkshire. Her parents, William and Augusta Peel, tragically also lost their son in the war. Major Home Peel DSO MC, of the 8th Battalion, London Regiment (Post Office Rifles) was killed in action on 24 March 1918 when Lesboeufs was lost to the Germans. He is buried in the Guards Cemetery in the French village of Lesboeufs.

Nurse Emily Hartman was born in Sheffield on 20 April 1895. During the First World War, she became a nurse in one of the Sheffield based VADs. She died of pneumonia on 20 October 1918 and is buried in the Ecclesfield Jewish Cemetery in Yorkshire. She had joined the VAD in April 1918, working initially in Manchester, before being transferred to the Bermondsey Military Hospital in London, where she contracted influenza. One of Emily's senior officers wrote to her parents after her death,

'I take a personal interest in all of our members, and knowing the splendid work done by Miss Hartman, I should like to convey my very deepest sympathy in your sad loss.'

Nurse Florence Hogg was 24 years old and a VAD nurse when she died of influenza on 31 October 1918. She is buried in the Horsforth Cemetery in Yorkshire.

Nurse Lady Beatrice Hilda Lever, wife of industrialist Sir Arthur Levy Lever, became a VAD nurse during the war. She died of septic poisoning whilst treating wounded British soldiers at the Hampstead General Hospital in London on 28 May 1917 and is buried in Golders Green Jewish Cemetery in London.

Nurse Edith Hilda Munro, aged 23, died on 12 December 1916. She was a nurse at the Dreadnought Seamen's Hospital in Greenwich, daughter of John Munro, a Scots engineer, and Leah Nathan, who was born in Bow. Edith was buried privately at Plashnet Jewish Cemetery, East Ham.

Nurse Ada Elizabeth Young was 33 when she died of influenza, pneumonia and cardiac failure on 15 July 1918. She had been nursing at Clipstone Camp Military Hospital since September 1917 and is buried in the churchyard of St Alban's, Forest Town. Her parents were Serjeant Major Young (5th Dragoon Guards) and Mrs Young of Dublin.

Nurse Lady Lelia Mathilda Samuelson, wife of Sir Bernhard Samuelson, 1st Bart, was 66 when she died 'of sickness' according to the CWGC register in France on 18 June 1915. She is buried in Dumbarton Cemetery.

Nurse Sophia Violet Barrett died 10 October 1918 when RMS *Leinster*, the Dun-Laoghaire to Holyhead mailboat, was torpedoed in the Irish Sea by submarine *UB-123*. She was returning to duty in France after being home on leave. She had been Mentioned in Despatches for her service. More than 500 people perished in the sinking which was the greatest single loss of life in the Irish Sea. After the recovery of Sophia's body, she was brought to Carrickmines House, County Galway where she had been staying and two days later her coffin was borne in an ambulance from Carrickmines to Kilternan, for burial. The cortege was headed by a mounted escort of Hussars.

Volunteer Eleanor Eileen Black died at sea on 4 June 1918 and is remembered on Hollybrook Memorial Southampton as her body was never recovered. She was travelling from South Africa to England on

RMS *Kenilworth Castle* when, 35 miles from Portsmouth, ships in the convoy collided and depth charges from one of them exploded under the *Kenilworth Castle*. Fifteen people on board were drowned, including several nurses.

Nurse Gertrude Annie Taylor, aged 34, had been serving with the 1st London General (TF) Hospital when she died of pneumonia in active service on 12 December 1916. She was one of about 2,000 Irish women who became VADS in the Great War. She was the daughter of Mr A. Taylor of Strandtown, Co. Down.

Nurse Meta Burgess, aged 35, died on the 31 January 1919. She had worked at No. 48 Stationary Hosital, Le Havre. The daughter of John and Elizabeth Burgess of Athlone, Co. Westmeath, she is buried in Dean's Grace Cemetery, Co Dublin.

Nurse Alice Amelia Potts, aged 50, died of influenza six days after the Armistice on 17 November 1918. She had worked at Aldridge Manor House in Walsall which was a medical facility between 1916 and 1919.

Member Barbara Esmee St John was 31 years of age and a member of the Sussex 112 Voluntary Aid Detachment, when she died on 12 October 1916 of Landry's Paralysis. She was buried with full military honours at the Communal Cemetery in Wimereux, 2 miles north of Boulogne, in the Pas de Calais region of France.

During the First World War, Cairo became a very crowded place with soldiers, nurses and refugees. The increased strain on an already over stretched sanitation system, was the main cause of the city being hit with cholera, typhoid and other similar epidemics. Some of the victims who are buried in Cairo War Memorial Cemetery are recorded here.

Worker S.J. Armstrong was a voluntary VAD worker, who died on 12 December 1918 whilst working in Egypt.

Nurse Lily Liddell was a nurse working for the VAD in Egypt as part of the London 250 detachment of the British Red Cross, when she died on 29 September 1918.

Nurse Marion Jane Maunsell was another VAD member who died on 7 January 1919.

Nursing Member P.G. Smyth died on 4 March 1919.

Worker M. Silva Stephenson died on 9 November 1915 whilst serving in Egypt.

Nursing Member Dorothy May Horrell died on 9 January 1921 whilst serving in Egypt and is buried in the Cairo New British Cemetery.

Nurse Helen Batchelor Taylor who was 42 years of age, worked for the VAD and was attached to the 4th Battalion, Bedfordshire Regiment who were stationed in Malta. She died of dysentery whilst working at the Floriana Hospital on 15 November 1915 and is buried in the Pieta Military Cemetery about a mile south of Valetta. The hospitals in Malta dealt with the tens of thousands of wounded British and Commonwealth soldiers, mainly from the fighting in Salonika and Gallipoli.

Helen B. Taylor (Courtesy of Alfie Beard).

Member Margaret Trevenen Arnold was 31 years of age and a member of the Surrey branch of the British Red Cross Voluntary Aid Detachment. After completing four months of initial training in England, she left for France on 5 June 1915 becoming one of the first VADs to serve in a military hospital overseas. On her arrival she found herself stationed at the 13th General Hospital in Le Tréport, in the Seine-Maritime region of France. Despite its status as a general hospital, all of the patients were accommodated in tents during their temporary stay. After contracting double pneumonia whilst working in an isolation ward, she was admitted to the Trianon Hospital on 10 March 1916 and on 12 March she died. She is buried in the Le Tréport Military Cemetery

Le Tréport was an important coastal town for Britain and her Allies. It was also home to the No. 3 General Hospital, which had been in place since November 1914, the No. 2 Canadian General Hospital, which arrived in March 1915, the No. 3 Convalescent Depot followed in June 1915. The following year saw the arrival of Lady Murray's British Red Cross Society Hospital. Collectively these hospitals could cater for 10,000 wounded soldiers. In March 1917, the No. 47 General Hospital arrived, and in the same year a divisional rest camp and a tank training depot were also added.

Member Nellie Taylor was 29 years of age and a member of the London/198 VAD, which she joined on 22 March 1917, and became attached to the 10th Motor Ambulance Convoy as a chauffeuse. Her VAD service card showed that she died on active service on 27 June 1918 aged 30, and is buried in the Mont Huon Military Cemetery at Le Tréport.

Member 14673 Edith Mary Tonkin was 26 years of age. Her home address was 32 Mill Road, Ely, West Cardiff, where she lived with her parents. She joined the London 250 VAD section as Member 14673 on 6 November 1917. She was sent out to France and served at the No. 3 General Hospital, which from November 1914 was situated at Le Tréport perched high up on a cliff overlooking the sea. The hospital was part of a tented location but also formed part of the Trianon Hotel. An entry for her on the Commonwealth War Graves Commission website shows that she 'died of disease' on 13 October 1918, and is buried in the Mont Huon Military Cemetery at Le Tréport.

Sister Amy Maud Augusta Parrott was 37 years old when she died on 24 October 1918 whilst serving in South Africa. She is buried in the Brixton Cemetery in Johannesburg. Her parents, Colonel and Mrs T.S. Parrott, lived in Sydney, Australia.

Nurse Jeannie Smith Lee, aged 25, joined the VAD and was attached to 30th Northumberland Detachment. She was sent out to France to work at the 9th General Hospital, which between November 1914 and June 1917, was at Rouen. The city was a major medical centre during the war and included eight General Hospitals, five Stationary Hospitals, a Red Cross Hospital, a Labour Hospital and No. 2 Convalescent Depot. Jeannie died of sickness on 30 March 1917 and is buried in the St Sever Cemetery, in Rouen. Her parents lived in Haltwhistle, in Northumberland.

Nurse Elizabeth McMath (Daisy) Warnock, aged 31, a nurse with the 10th Glasgow VAD, was attached to the 8th General Hospital in Rouen when she died of septicaemia on 5 May 1918. She is buried in the St Sever Cemetery in Rouen. Her parents, William and Mary Warnock, lived at 19 Westminster Terrace, in Glasgow.

Elizabeth's brother, Lieutenant George Muir Warnock, was 25 years old and serving in the 8th Battalion (Princess Louise's) Argyll and Sutherland Highlanders, a Territorial unit, when he died of his wounds just five weeks before his sister, on 29 March 1918. He was also buried in the St Sever Cemetery in Rouen. By a strange twist of fate, he was admitted to the 8th General Hospital, where his sister worked. He was wounded on 21 March 1918, the first day of the German Spring Offensive, whilst operating as a Lewis machine-gun officer on the Somme. It is inconceivable that Elizabeth would not have been aware of his presence in the hospital, and no doubt she would have been able to attend his funeral.

One of George's senior officers, Major Lockie wrote the following letter to George's mother: 'George was one of the bravest and best boys I ever knew, was most lovable and always had a ready smile no matter what was happening; was my most able and willing assistant in many things when I was Second in Command of the Battalion, and I loved him as I did my own son. I have seen your son in battle, and never was anyone so keen to do his duty. His conduct in and out of the line was absolutely beyond reproach; he was a very gallant and true gentleman.'

Another officer, Major Moir wrote. 'Your son was a very great loss, not only as a friend but as a very fine officer. During the Cambrai battle he was the only officer left in headquarters with me, and he did magnificently, I cannot speak too highly of his work throughout.'

He was Mentioned in Despatches by General Sir Douglas Haig, in the *London Gazette* on 7 April 1918 for gallant and distinguished service in the field.

Nurse 5719 Mabel Elizabeth Chadwick, stationed at the 17th General Hospital in Alexandria, died of enteric fever on 15 October 1915. She is buried in the Alexandria (Chatby) Military and War Memorial Cemetery. Her mother, Mrs Elizabeth Ann Chadwick, lived at 16 Hobart Street, Leicester.

Nurse 5540 Gertrude Lucinda Roskell, aged 38 and also stationed at the 17th General Hospital in Alexandria, died on 31 October of acute appendicitis. She was buried in the same cemetery as her colleague Mabel Chadwick. Gertrude hailed from Knebworth in Hertfordshire.

Nurse 5725 Florence Emily Smales was 38 years old when she died on 13 October 1915 whilst stationed at the 19th General Hospital in Alexandria, Egypt. She is also buried in the Alexandria (Chatby) Military and War Memorial Cemetery. In England she lived with her parents, sisters and brother at Magdale Place, Whitby in Yorkshire. The family were affluent and had four servants to look after them.

Sister Madeline Elsie Bates was 35 years old when she died on 22 December 1917. She had been working in France as part of the Millicent Sutherland Ambulance Service in Calais and had been granted a

Headstone of Madeline Elsie Bates.

period of home leave as she had been diagnosed as suffering with shell shock. Tragically, while at home recovering, she was caught in a German air raid and died of her wounds. She is buried in St Mary the Virgin Parish Church at Shenfield, Essex.

Nurse Mrs Alicia Palmieri was part of the Joint War Committee. According to the Commonwealth War Graves Commission website, she died on 15 May 1917, aged 45, whilst in hospital at Petrograd, Russia. Her name is commemorated on the Archangel Memorial, on the eastern side of the Dvina Estuary, on the White Sea. A photograph of Alicia, in her nurse's attire, is held by the Imperial War Museum. According to information posted on the Great War Forum, this courageous woman trained at New York City Hospital and was later superintendent of the Yellow Fever Hospital in Havana, Cuba. In 1915 she nursed typhus patients in Serbia 'under conditions calculated to daunt the bravest' before moving to France and then in 1916 to a Russo-Serbian unit in Petrograd.

Nursing Sister Cicely Mary Leigh Pope was 31 years of age when she died of influenza on 25 June 1921. She is buried in the Cheka Kula Military Cemetery in Serbia.

Nurse Margaret Caroline C. Ryle was 23 years of age and a VAD nurse attached to the Russian Red Cross, when she died on 21 February 1915. She is also buried in the Cheka Kula Military Cemetery in Serbia. Her home was at 15 German Place, Brighton, Sussex, where before the war she had lived with her parents Reginald and Catherine Ryle, and her nine other siblings, five brothers and four sisters. Her father, Reginald, was a doctor, which perhaps influenced her vocation.

Nursing Sister Catherine Ball was 28 years of age and working at Alexandria Hospital in Egypt when she died. She was on board HMS *Osmanieh*, when the ship struck a mine on 31 December 1917, and sank at the entrance of the harbour. The vessel ran weekly trips between Malta and Mudros during the Gallipoli campaign, usually with mail and supplies, but sometimes her cargo would be troops and medical staff. The mine had been laid by the German submarine *UC-34*. In total 3 officers, 21 crew members, 167 troops and 8 nurses, all lost their lives in the tragedy.

Catherine is buried in the Alexandria (Hadra) War Memorial Cemetery. Her home was at 25 Trent Bridge Footway, Nottingham, where she lived with her parents, John and Catherine Ball. She had started working for the VAD in October 1915, and before going out to work in Alexandria, she had worked at VAD at Arnott Hill Hospital, Bowden Hospital, and

Lakenham Military Hospital. Six of her colleagues also lost their lives and are buried in Alexandria (Hadra) War Memorial Cemetery.

Nursing Sister Winifred Maud Brown, aged 30, also from Nottingham.

Nurse Gertrude Bytheway, aged 37 and from Walsall in Staffordshire.

Nurse Lilian Midwood, aged 32 and from London.

Nurse Hermione Angela Rogers, aged 22.

Nurse Una Marguerite Duncanson was another of the nurses who drowned when the *Osmanieh* sank on 31 December 1917. She lived at Langley Park Farm, Langley Maidstone, Kent, with her parents, James and Annie Duncanson, and her seven brothers and sisters.

Her elder brother, Second Lieutenant Roy Duncanson, 3rd Battalion, Duke of Wellington's (West Riding) Regiment, attached to the 9th Battalion, was killed in action on 7 July 1916, a week in to the Battle of the Somme. He has no known grave and his name is commemorated on the Thiepval Memorial which is situated in the Somme region of France.

Her younger brother, Second Lieutenant Ian Ferguson Duncanson, 8th Battalion, (Princess Louise's) Argyll & Sutherland Highlanders had been killed in action just eleven weeks before his sister, on 12 October 1917. He is buried in the Poelcapelle British Cemetery, which is situated in the West-Vlaanderen region of Belgium.

The eldest sibling, Fergus Duncanson also served during the war, as a Private (S/12973) with the Black Watch (Royal Highlanders). He survived the war and lived to be 90 years of age, passing away in 1980.

Nurse Marion Dorothy Chapman was 27 years of age and a nurse with the Durham No. 2 section VAD. She was working at the 17th General Hospital in Alexandria when she died on 10 August 1918. She had served with the VAD since enlisting with them on 3 January 1917. She was buried in the Alexandria (Hadra) War Memorial Cemetery. She lived with her parents at 'Seacroft', Westoe, South Shields.

Nursing Sister Dorothea Mary Lynette Crewdson was 32 years of age and a Nursing Sister with the VAD when she 'died of disease' on 12 March 1919 whilst serving at one of the hospitals at Etaples, France. She was buried in the nearby Etaples Military Cemetery, and was a holder of the Military Medal awarded for gallantry and devotion to duty during an enemy air raid. The *London Gazette* citation records: 'Although herself wounded this lady remained at duty and assisted in dressing the wounds of patients.'

Nursing Sister 541 Alice Violet Hallam was 45 years of age and a member of the London 114 Voluntary Aid Detachment attached to the 18th General Hospital at Etaples in France. She had begun working for the VAD on 2 June 1915 and continued to do so until her death from illness contracted on duty, whilst still in service in France, on 18 December 1916. She is buried in the Etaples Military Cemetery.

Member Margaret Ellen Evans was 39 years of age and attached to the 83rd General Hospital, in the small French town of Wimereux, about 2 miles north of Boulogne, when she died on 22 July 1917. She is buried in Wimereux Communal Cemetery, in the Pas de Calais region of France.

Member Nita Madeline King was 29 years old and serving in France at one of the numerous military hospitals to be found at Etaples, when she died on 25 May 1917. She is buried in the Wimereux Communal Cemetery. Her family were from Cosham in Hampshire.

Nurse Florence Mary Faithfull, who lived at 26 Upper Redlands Road, Reading, Berkshire, enlisted in the Hampshire 194 section of the VAD on 28 July 1917 when she was 24 years old. At the time of her death through drowning on 15 January 1918, she was attached to the 65th British General Hospital. There is a slight confusion in relation to Florence, as the Commonwealth War Graves Commission has her having been buried in the Basra War Cemetery in what was then Mesopotamia, latter day Iraq, whilst her VAD Service card shows her as serving at a British Military Hospital in Salonica.

Member Ellen Caroline Meares was 44 years old when she died on 24 February 1919. She is buried in the Brookwood Military Cemetery in Surrey. Her VAD Service Card records that she was only 36 years of age when she died although the CWGC entry gives her age as 44. Both sources show that she lived at the same address, 4 Bushmead Avenue, Bedford. She commenced her service with the VAD on 23 February 1916 and worked at the 4th London General Hospital at Denmark Hill. In April 1917 she volunteered for overseas service and was sent out to France where she was attached to a French military hospital. She returned to the 4th London General Hospital, Maudsley Section, on 4 December 1917, where she stayed until 22 February 1919, dying two days later.

Nurse Aileen W. Powers-Peel was born in Toronto in 1894 and was 24 at the time of her death on 31 December 1918. During the war, Aileen did secretarial work for the Canadian Red Cross Headquarters and was also qualified as a chauffeuse. One of forty-seven Canadian nurses who died during the First World War, she is buried in Brookwood Military Cemetery in Surrey.

Driver Miss Lilian Beatrice Nichols was 33 years of age when she died of pneumonia on 1 March 1919. She is buried in the Brookwood Military Cemetery in Surrey. Her parents were Eliza Jane William and Arthur Nichols.

Volunteer Wilmet Annie Bennett was 32 years of age and a New Zealander by birth. She died of appendicitis on 21 November 1918 and is buried in the Walton-on-Thames Cemetery in Surrey. It is more than likely that Wilmet would have been working at the No. 2 New Zealand General Hospital at the time of her death, which was at Mount Felix, Walton-on-Thames, Surrey.

Nurse 83/M/274 Phyllis May Maltby was 27 years of age when she died of pneumonia on 6 December 1918. She is buried in the Brookwood Military Cemetery in Surrey. Her late father was Lieutenant Colonel Francis Grant Maltby of the Indian army.

Nurse Isabel Lois Harding was 22 when she died of pneumonia on 8 April 1917. She had joined the VAD as a nurse on 27 November 1918, and was then allocated to work at the 1st Southern General Hospital in Birmingham. Isabel died of pneumonia on 15 February 1919 and was buried in Lodge Hill Cemetery in Birmingham. She was the daughter of George and Elizabeth Annie Harding of Branganstown, Kilcock, Co. Kildare.

Nurse Mary Agnes Langdale died on 9 February 1917, aged 39. She was the daughter of Arthur and Catherine de Bruyn Langdale, of 45 Church Rd, Barnes, London and is buried in Tidworth Military Cemetery.

Nurse Grace Errol Bolton died of pneumonia contracted on duty on 16 February 1919. She was 28 and the daughter of J.W. and Annie E. Bolton of Montreal, Quebec and is buried in Montreal (Mount Royal) Cemetery.

Nurse Lilian Kate Jones was killed in action on 6 June 1916 and is buried in Newport (St Woolos) Cemetery.

Nurse Florence Hilda Chadwick died of illness contracted on duty on 2 November 1918 and is buried in St Alban's (Hatfield Road) Cemetery.

Nurse B.A. Lambarde, the daughter of William and Florence Lambarde, of Bradbourne Hall, Sevenoaks, died on 5 March 1919 aged 29. She served at the Royal Naval Hospital, Portsmouth and is buried in Riverhead (St Mary) Churchyard.

Nurse Margaret Alice Baron from Clayton-le-Moors in Lancashire succumbed to influenza and died in the military hospital in Deal on 22 October 1918, aged 28. Originally a weaver, she had nursed since the beginning of the war and was buried in the cemetery of her home town.

Nurse Mary Ann Eliza Young died of pneumonia contracted on duty on 13 February 1919. She was 35 and the daughter of John and Mercy Young, of 7, Machen Place Riverside, Cardiff. Prior to volunteering she had been an assistant mistress at Lansdowne Rd Council School, Cardiff. She is buried in the Mazargues War Cemetery, Marseilles.

Volunteer Elizabeth Marjory (Elma) Gordon was 43 when she died on 11 September 1917. The daughter of General William Gordon, CIE and Harriet Elizabeth Gordon, of Banffshire, she is buried in Mikra British Cemetery, Kalamaria.

Volunteer Gladys Maud Jones, the daughter of Alfred and Adelaide Letitia Jones, of The Spinney, Great Shelford, Cambridge died on 21 August 1917 aged 31. She is buried in Mikra British Cemetery, Kalamaria.

Nurse Ella Richards, aged 31, died on 14 October 1918 and is buried in Mikra British Cemetery, Kalamaria. She had served in hospitals in France and Salonika. In *The Nurses War: the Red Cross in Salonika in WWI* author Loretta Proctor writes: 'Sadly, just before she was due to return home, Ella succumbed to the outbreak of pneumonia and influenza that swept through the exhausted nurses and officers at the end of the war. A memorial plaque was erected for her at Soar Congregational Chapel in Lampeter, Wales by the children of her Sunday School class.'

Nurse Mabel Olive Craggs died on 20 January 1915 and is buried in the Levallois-Perret Communal Cemetery, Paris.

Nurse Mary C. Dickson, aged 30, died on 16 February 1917. She was the daughter of the Rev. W.A. and Mary Dickson, of Shedagh, Fahan, Donegal, and is buried in St Sever Cemetery, Rouen.

Nurse Mary Cawston Bousfield, aged 27, was working at the 8th General Hospital in Rouen when she died of illness contracted on duty on 24 February 1919. The daughter of William G.R. and Mary Bousfield, of 26, Gwendolen Avenue, Putney Hill, London, she had been Mentioned in Despatches for her work.

Nurse Gwynedd Violet Llewellyn died of influenza aged 19 on 3 November 1918. She had only been at the British Red Cross Hospital based in Rouen for twelve days and is buried in St Sever Cemetery Extension, Rouen. She was the daughter of Lieutenant Colonel A. Llewellyn OBE and Mrs. A. Llewellyn, of Wribbenhal, Bewdley, Worcestershire.

Nurse Katharine Ferrars Kinnear, aged 29, died on 3 September 1917 and is buried in Malo-lès-Bains Communal Cemetery. She was the daughter of the Rev. and Mrs Henry G. Kinnear, M.A., and was born at Ripon, Yorks. She was awarded a Diploma by the French Government in recognition of her services.

Nurse W. Bailey died on 23 September 1918 and is buried in Staglieno Cemetery, Genoa.

Worker Annie Neish died on 18 October 1918, aged 32. She was the daughter of William Neish, of 'Elem', Pilford Heath, Wimbourne, Dorset.

Nursing Sister Ida Thekla Bowser died on 11 January 1919, aged 45, and is buried in Hastings Cemetery. Born in Marylebone, London, she had been a nurse since 1902 and was the author of *Britain's Civilian Volunteers; Authorized Story of British Voluntary Aid Detachment Work in the Great War*. She was awarded the Order of St John of Jerusalem for her work.

Nurse Audrey Heritage, a former Girl Guide, was just 17 when she died on 31 October 1918. She came from Little Common, Bexhill-on-Sea and had been nursing at St John's VAD Hospital (Holmesdale Gardens). A diary extract from a colleague recorded that during the influenza epidemic 'she remained on duty when so many were stricken that the nursing staff were sadly depleted. At last off duty, she went to bed sick and tired and was found next morning – called to higher service. She was buried with full military honours in the hero's corner at the Borough Cemetery.'

Nurse Venice Clementine Henrietta Hackett was one of three siblings to die during the war who were the children of Edward and Emilie Hackett, of Castletown Park, Ballycumber. Venice died of influenza and pneumonia on 13 October 1918, at the height of the influenza pandemic, and is buried in Ballycumber (Liss) Churchyard. Her brothers were Captain Learo A.H. Hacket MC who was killed in action on 24 April 1918 and Second Lieutenant Eric A.N. Hackett who was killed in action on 9 September 1916.

Nurse Edith Frances Barker, aged 49, was the daughter of Richard and Emily Barker, of Huyton, Liverpool. She had worked in Malta in 1915 but was invalided home with dysentery. In 1917 she went to France and, following a period of leave, returned in March 1918. She was taken ill and died suddenly on 3 April in St Omer and is buried in Longuenesse (St Omer) Souvenir Cemetery.

Nursing Member Elizabeth Thomson was killed by a bomb from an enemy aircraft on 30 September 1917 and is buried in Longuenesse (St Omer) Souvenir Cemetery.

Member Daisy Kathleen Mary Coles, aged 24, was the daughter of Mr and Mrs Walter G. Coles, of Priorsford House, Peebles. She was working at the 58 (Scottish) General Hospital and was presumably killed in the same way as Elizabeth Thomson on 30 September 1917. She too is buried in Longuenesse (St Omer) Souvenir Cemetery. She had been Mentioned in Despatches.

Nurse Jennie Williams, aged 45, was the daughter of John and Ellen Williams, of Plas Coch, Llanberis, Carnarvonshire. She was buried in Ste Marie Cemetery, Le Havre.

Nurse Edith Ingram, aged 31, daughter of Mrs. S A. Ingram, of Clymping, Littlehampton, was killed during an air raid on the 55th General Hospital near Boulogne on 14 August 1918. She is is buried in Terlincthun British Cemetery, Wimille, France.

Nurse Margaret Cameron Young, aged 25, daughter of Amelia and the late Thomas Young, of 37, Newington Avenue, Belfast died of illness on 30 July 1918 and is also buried in Terlincthun British Cemetery, Wimille, France.

CHAPTER EIGHT

QUEEN MARY AND PRINCESS MARY

No book about women in the Great War would really be complete without including a piece about Queen Mary and Princess Mary, the wife and daughter of King George V, who was the British monarch throughout the entirety of the First World War.

Queen Mary was born, Victoria Mary Augusta Louise Olga Pauline Claudine Agnes, on 26 May 1867 at Kensington Palace in London, but was affectionately known by the name 'May' after the month in which she was born.

Mary was due to marry Prince Albert Victor, but he died suddenly of influenza on 14 January 1892, only six weeks after proposing marriage to her on 3 December 1891. The wedding was set for 27 February 1892. After Albert's death, Prince George and Mary shared their grief for him, which over a period of time brought them closer together, they fell in love and he proposed to her the following year. Some historians claimed Albert was connected with the 'Jack the Ripper' murders, although nothing was ever conclusively proved against him.

She married, the then Prince George, Duke of York, on 6 July 1893, in the Chapel Royal at St James Palace, London. After their wedding they set up home in a property on the Sandringham estate in Norfolk. Their marriage produced six children, Princess Mary, and five sons, Princes Albert, Edward, George, Henry and John.

George became king on 6 May 1910 after the death of his father, Edward VII. He sat side by side with Victoria Mary on the occasion of her Coronation on 22 June 1911, at which time she chose to use her second name, Mary, out of respect for the memory of Queen Victoria.

Queen Mary engrossed herself fully in helping the war effort on the home front and by setting an example to an entire nation who looked up to her, King George and the British Royal Family. At the outbreak of the war she introduced austerity measures at Buckingham Palace by the rationing of food for both her family and members of staff. Once wounded servicemen started returning to the UK, King George, Queen Mary and

Queen Mary and Princess Mary.

their daughter, Princess Mary, journeyed to numerous military hospitals to visit them and pass on their gratitude and that of a grateful nation.

On 10 August 1914, with the war less than a week old, the following article appeared in the *Daily Mirror* newspaper concerning an appeal which had been made on behalf of Queen Mary. It would not be the last such appeal she would make during the course of the following four years.

CALL TO THE WOMEN
Queen Mary's Appeal to Needleworkers to
Make Garments for Sufferers

Queen Mary appeals to the women of Britain to assist in making garments for those who will suffer on account of the war.

Her Majesty has asked the Presidents of needlework guilds throughout the British Isles to organise a large collection of garments; the Queen said:-

'I hope that the guilds will co-operate with the Prince of Wales's National Relief Fund, with the Red Cross Society, who have the organising of working parties among their schemes, the Territorial Associations and the Soldiers and Sailors Help Society.

The most useful garments for soldiers and sailors on active service are, flannel shirts, socks, sweaters and cardigan jackets, flannel bed jackets and bed socks, which would be distributed by the British Red Cross Society.

Large numbers of all the ordinary garments for women and children will be required.

Those garments intended for persons suffering from distress owing to unemployment should be sent to the Committee for the Prevention and Relief and Distress which are being formed by the mayors and provosts and the chairmen of the county councils and larger urban district councils.

It should be remembered that all flannel garments should be made in a large size, and suitable paper patterns can be obtained from Butterick, 175 Regent Street.'

One of the numerous other appeals Queen Mary made was in aid of the Work for Women Fund. Amazingly after she made an appeal on the Fund's behalf in national newspapers in early September 1914, £20,000 was donated in just one day. This included two donations of £5,000 each, which were staggering amounts of money for the time. This showed just how much the royal family were revered at the time by the public. It is highly unlikely that such a large sum of money would have been raised without Queen Mary's request and support. During the course of the war, she made many similar appeals for a plethora of good causes which helped raise hundreds of thousands of pounds, which otherwise would not have been raised.

It was not just the support and assistance she gave to the people and the nation as a whole, but the continued support she gave to the king, nearly always by his side when he was carrying out official appointments. The solidity of their relationship, a mirror of their love for one another, must have resonated positively with their loyal subjects.

It is only when one reads through newspaper articles in relation to Queen Mary that the real scope of the part she played in the First World War can truly be appreciated. Hardly a day went by without her being mentioned in some way, either in relation to the numerous charitable funds she supported and helped raise much needed monies for, or by the visits she made to wounded soldiers in hospitals across the United Kingdom, or by the number of official functions she attended in company with her husband – a truly remarkable woman. Sadly, Prince John, who was the youngest of her six children, died on 18 January 1919 of a severe seizure, at Wood Farm, Sandringham. He was just 13 years of age.

There were many buildings and organisations named after Queen Mary including Queen Mary's Royal Naval Hospital at the Palace Hotel in Southend-on-Sea, Essex that could cater for 400 patients. The premises had been donated rent free for the duration of the war by the family of the late Mr Alfred Tolhurst. There was a battle cruiser of the British Royal Navy with the name, the *Queen Mary*. It was sunk on 31 May 1916 at the Battle of Jutland with the loss of 1,266 of her crew. Sadly there were only twenty survivors. There were three army regiments that had Queen Mary in the title as well as the Queen Mary Army Auxiliary Corps.

In 1918, Queen Mary became the Patron of the Women's Army Auxiliary Corps, and in keeping with the importance of her patronage the name of the organisation was changed to Queen Mary's Army Auxiliary Corps. Between 1918 and when it was disbanded in 1920, 57,000 women had served with the Corps.

Princess Mary, the king and queen's only daughter, was 17 years of age at the outbreak of the war, and in November 1914, she was responsible for organising the Soldiers and Sailors Christmas Fund. At the same time an advert was placed in national newspapers inviting financial donations to be sent in to the fund, to provide every member of His Majesty's armed forces, who was serving overseas on Christmas Day, with a festive gift.

Not surprisingly, the response from the public was overwhelming. The decision was taken to provide each man who met the criteria of entitlement, with an embossed brass tin, the contents of which varied depending

Princess Mary Christmas Tin, 1914.

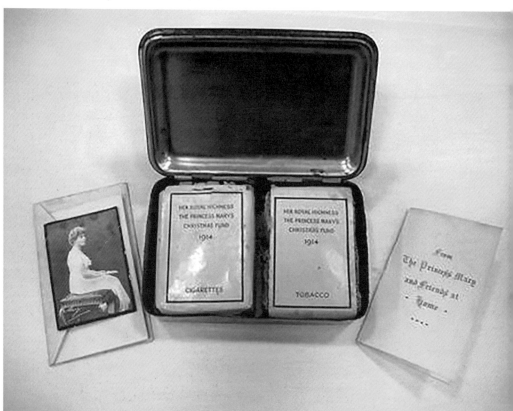

Bullet pencil included in the tin.

A card from the king and queen (Army version).

A Corporal from a British Cavalry unit opening his tin (Supplement to the *Auckland Weekly News*, 25/2/1915).

on who you were. The contents for officers and men consisted of a pipe, a lighter, twenty cigarettes, and some loose tobacco. The tins intended for nurses contained chocolate while those for non-smokers and boys contained a pencil that looked like a .303 bullet. The bullet pulled out of the cartridge case to reveal the other end which was a pencil. For them there was also a packet of sweets. Indian troops received sweets and spices in their tins.

Each of the tins was embossed with a sideways view of Princess Mary, and the names of Britain's Allies were engraved down both sides of the front of the tin. They each contained a card with a picture of the king and queen. The king had a different uniform in his picture depending on whether the tin was for a soldier or sailor.

Queen and Princess Mary in 1918 (Photograph by Bain News Service).

On the reverse of each of the cards was the king's greeting to his military personnel which said, 'May God protect you and bring you home safely.'

Enough money was raised by the campaign, nearly £200,000, to pay for more than 2.5 million of the tins and their contents, although only 350,000 of them had been delivered by Christmas Day.

In June 1918 Princess Mary started a nursing course at the Great Ormond Street Hospital in London, where she worked for two days a week on the Alexandra ward, she also worked tirelessly promoting the Girl Guides, VADs and the Land Girls, as well as visiting wounded soldiers in hospital with her mother throughout the war.

CONCLUSION

As can be seen from the evidence, women played an extremely important role during the First World War, both on the home front and in different theatres of war across the world, and that their efforts continued throughout the conflict.

Early on in the war the British authorities, under the guise of the Wartime Propaganda Bureau, used poster campaigns to assist with different aspects of the conflict, but nearly all of them involved women and children to some degree. Some of the posters were aimed at men, but appealed to them in different ways. For example, after what was referred to in the press as the 'Rape of Belgium', a term that was coined at the time to describe the overall behaviour of German soldiers towards the Belgium civilian population in the early weeks of the war, posters of women and their children were used to encourage men to enlist so that they could make sure the same didn't happen to their own loved ones should the unthinkable occur and Britain also be invaded.

Other posters were used to encourage women to try and persuade their men folk to enlist in the armed forces, and to challenge them as to why they hadn't done so. Some were aimed directly at women in an attempt to persuade getting them to join one of the many voluntary organisations which had sprung up following the outbreak of the war, of which there were many.

Women carried this country in so many different ways during the war, especially on the home front with the work they did in covering the roles that men had previously filled. Add to this the voluntary work which they so willingly undertook, many whilst having to work, look after and care for their children and their home, whilst spending lonely nights wondering if they would ever again see their loved ones who had gone off to war.

For those in the nursing and support services, it can only be guessed how many lives they were responsible for helping to save, how many times they made a dying man's final moments less lonely or how they risked and often lost their own lives in the service of others. Thankfully women didn't have to fight in the war and die in the trenches, but the supportive work which they continually undertook throughout the war, was definitely a game changer.

As well as the almost 750,000 men who died in the war, we also owe a great debt to this past generation of fantastic women, who should also be remembered each year on Remembrance Day Sunday.

SOURCES &
ACKNOWLEDGEMENTS

The Great War Forum
hastingsforum.co.uk
www.ancestry.co.uk
www.cwgc.co.uk
Wikipedia
www.qaranc.co.uk
www.ags.bucks.sch.uk
www.nursingmemorialappeal.org.uk
www.historyanswers.co.uk
www.stephen-stratford.co.uk
www.qarns.co.uk
www.uboat.net
www.mersyside-at-war.org
www.ournottinghamshire.org.uk
www.findmygrave.com
www.wartimememoriesproject.com
www.invisionzone.com
www.redcross.org.uk
forum.gallipoli-association.org
www.eastbelfastww1.com
Ainsdale at War Memorial, by Bruce Hubbard.
www.britishnewspaperarchive.co.uk
www.spartacus-educational.com
www.1914-1918.invisionzone.com
www.womenslandarmy.co.uk
www.accringtonobserver.co.uk
http://rememberingfirstworldwarnurses.blogspot.co.uk
The Nurses War: the Red Cross in Salonika in WWI, by Loretta Proctor
The Flaming Sword: In Serbia and Elsewhere, by Mabel Anne St Clair Stobart (Hodder and Stoughton)
Irene Moore for her helpful and thoughtful assistance in the editing of this book.

INDEX